The Fine Art of Art Security

PROTECTING PUBLIC AND PRIVATE COLLECTIONS AGAINST THEFT, FIRE, AND VANDALISM

Donald L. Mason

 VAN NOSTRAND REINHOLD COMPANY
New York Cincinnati Toronto London Melbourne

To my family

Copyright © 1979 by Litton Educational Publishing, Inc.
Library of Congress Catalog Card Number 78-14894
ISBN 0-442-25118-1

Printed in United States of America.

Designed by Loudan Enterprises

Published in 1979 by Van Nostrand Reinhold Company
A division of Litton Educational Publishing, Inc.
135 West 50th Street, New York, NY 10001, U.S.A.

Van Nostrand Reinhold Limited
1410 Birchmount Road
Scarborough, Ontario M1P 2E7, Canada

Van Nostrand Reinhold Australia Pty. Ltd.
17 Queen Street
Mitcham, Victoria 3132, Australia

Van Nostrand Reinhold Company Limited
Molly Millars Lane
Wokingham, Berkshire, England

16 15 14 13 12 11 10 9 8 7 6 5 4 3 2 1

Library of Congress Cataloging in Publication Data
Mason, Donald L
   The fine art of art security.

   Includes index.
    1. Art—Protection. 2. Art museum—Security measures. 3. Art galleries, Commercial—Security measures. I. Title.
N463.M37   069'.54   78-14894
ISBN 0-442-25118-1

Contents

Introduction

During the past fifteen years, one might say that interest in art has kept pace with the spiral of inflation. By the same token, the art thief has taken a ride on that very spiral.

How did it all commence? Some say it all seemed to come into focus when, in November, 1961, the Metropolitan Museum of Art purchased Rembrandt's magnificent oil painting *Aristotle Contemplating the Bust of Homer* for $2,300,000. It was the very first painting to be purchased for a sum in excess of one million dollars. The sale made headlines throughout the world and what followed was a golden era, where art prices broke record after record. The press covered this phenomenon with generous portions of publicity. The notoriety resulted in an attendance increase at galleries, auction houses, and museums; the notoriety also triggered the nefarious mind of the art thief and he acted.

While it is true that art thefts are nothing new, the recent statistics on art thefts are staggering. In 1974 Italy reported nearly eleven thousand art thefts; France reported sixty-five hundred; and England, the United States, and other nations have problems of similar proportions. The art thefts in France increased fifteen to twenty percent during the period between 1970 and 1974 alone. Even the museums, the traditional strongholds of art collections, have not been immune. In a survey recently conducted, the International Foundation for Art Research determined that seventy-five percent of the reporting museums in the United States and Canada had suffered at least one theft in the five years past. Estimates of the total value of stolen art throughout the world go as high as one billion dollars. Needless to say, insurance rates have kept pace with the tremendous increase in art thefts. In fact, the high rates have caused some museums to actually cancel exhibitions.

International concern about the art theft problem is at a feverish level. During the November, 1973 UNESCO Conference on Art Theft and Other Forms of Illicit Transfer of Ownership, held in Belgium, an Interpol (International Criminal Police Organization) survey concerning the problems of vandalism and art theft was discussed. The survey, to which thirty-seven countries replied, concluded that: (a) the great majority of thefts occur in public or private places where there is no system of technical protection or where the system of protection is insufficient; (b) cultural property of great artistic and commercial value is recovered more easily than items of lesser value which are more easily negotiated; (c) in the great majority of cases of cultural property which has been recovered, professionals in the art trade (secondhand dealers, retailers, antique dealers, etc.) have, at one time or another, been concerned; (d) there is more international traffic in stolen art objects between neighboring countries, while the market for such objects is generally located in large cities.

Several of the experts remarked that, among the perils threatening cultural property, vandalism must, in certain respects, be considered in a distinct way. While in fact certain measures for the protection of art works are effective for both theft and vandalism, thieves and vandals have profoundly different motivations. The result is that the mere fear of repression—which might have a certain effectiveness with regard to theft—is ineffective where vandalism is concerned. The preventive measures must be different, since they must aim at doing away with different kinds of motivations.[1]

The art thief is active wherever a country's artistic achievements have been proven to be marketable. He has stolen art objects from archaeological diggings, caves, temples, cathedrals, museums, galleries, homes, libraries, schools, and other institutions. He has often stolen art while it was being transported. He is not always a careful worker and in the excitement he often damages his loot. It is not uncommon for the investigator to find that the thief has used a sharp instrument to cut a painting out of its frame. One thief cut an ancient Mayan stela into eight pieces so that natives could transport the pieces through the jungle to a small aircraft for shipment to another country. Another thief left a painting hidden in the woods with little protection against the weather; the exposure caused it to crumble

1. "Theft of Cultural Property: A Report by the Interpol General Secretariat to the Organization's Forty-Second General Assembly," *Museum* (quarterly review published by UNESCO) XXVI No. 1 (1974): 4–7.

in his hands when he tried to retrieve the painting several weeks later. Sadly, that painting is lost to mankind forever.

Some stolen paintings become international travellers. In 1936, during a battle in the Spanish Civil War, an El Greco canvas modello, called *The Immaculate Conception*, was stolen from the wall of a villa outside Madrid, Spain. The thief transported the painting to Mexico and then to Los Angeles, California. Ultimately, the painting found its way to New York City, where the author recovered it in June, 1971. After four years of litigation, the painting was returned to the villa from which it had been stolen thirty-nine years before. (Figure 1.)

Most art thefts are performed by the sneak thief or the burglar, but the use of violence to commit art theft is also becoming a more common occurrence.

For example, in 1972 the Montreal Museum of Fine Arts was robbed of eighteen oil paintings, valued collectively at two million dollars. Three masked individuals, armed with sawed-off shotguns, gained entrance to the building via one of the skylights and slid down a rope to the floor below. They bound and gagged three security guards. (Figures 2, 3, and 4.)

Interestingly, the skylight was also the burglars' point of entry into the Pitti Palace Museum in Florence, Italy in April of 1978. After breaking through the skylight, the thieves used a rope ladder to lower themselves into the museum. They stole ten paintings, the most important of which was Rubens' masterpiece *The Three Graces*, a 23- by 14-inch (58.4- by 35.6-cm) monochrome on wood. A successful daytime theft took place in April, 1975 when a Rembrandt painting was carried out of the Boston Museum of Fine Arts by two armed men. On February 1, 1976 three armed men overpowered guards at the Papal Palace in Avignon, France, and stole 119 paintings by Pablo Picasso. On January 29, 1978 and February 20, 1978 thieves entered the art museum in St. Louis, Missouri by smashing a glass window and door with a sledge hammer. Among the art objects stolen were a Frederic Remington bronze statue, called *Bronco Buster*, and three Auguste Rodin bronze statues. . . . The list of robberies goes on and on.

In addition to the violence committed in the theft of art, man, in his madness, has lashed out and damaged such famous works of art as Michelangelo's *Pieta* at St. Peter's in Rome, Italy, and Picasso's gigantic work *Guernica* at the Museum of Modern Art in New York.

Figure 1. El Greco's *The Immaculate Conception* was stolen from a Spanish villa during the Spanish Civil War. Photographed by Dr. C. Gregory Caltabiano.

In recent years law enforcement agencies throughout the world have gathered strong evidence to indicate that organized crime is involved in the theft and sale of stolen art objects. The tentacles of organized crime tend to stick wherever an item can be sold for a sizable profit; stolen art is one such item.

My own involvement in this problem is unique. Up to my retirement in August, 1976, I was the FBI's (Federal Bureau of Investigation's) senior art theft and art fraud investigator. During the first eight years of my eleven-year period of duty in this area, I was the

Figure 2. Jeunne Fille Accoudee sur le Bras Gauche by Jeanne-Baptiste-Camille Corot. Bequest of Miss Olive Hosmer. This oil painting was one of eighteen stolen from the Montreal Museum of Fine Arts in 1972.

only FBI agent whose exclusive assignment it was to investigate art crimes. Although my office of assignment was in New York City, my investigations of art cases took me throughout the United States and abroad.

I have seen grief etched in the faces of art thief victims whose treasures took a lifetime to acquire. I have seen embarrassed gallery and museum personnel and, similarly, collectors, who, through carelessness, contributed to the successful theft of an art object or an entire collection. I was often appalled to find that the victim had had

Figure 3.   Portrait of Brigadier General Sir Robert Fletcher by Thomas Gainsborough, R.A. Bequest of Miss Olive Hosmer. One of the paintings stolen from the Montreal Museum of Fine Arts. The thieves gained access to the museum through a skylight.

absolutely no security system at all. One gallery had but a single lock on the front door to protect over one million dollars worth of art.

Prior to writing this book, I was primarily involved in the recovery of art works and the prosecution of persons involved in the theft. This book takes me in a new direction; that is, the science of art security. It has not been my intention to endorse any product described herein, but, rather to present the system to the reader for his consideration, just as the manufacturer presented it to me. I have seen a good portion of the security systems that are described in this book in operation. With the rapid advances being made in this technology, it should be noted that even newer systems will probably be on the market before this book is published.

While I have been very impressed by the range of electronic equipment available in this field, I also recognize the importance of a well-trained and efficient guard force where it is feasible and highly recommend it.

This book presents a wide variety of highly sophisticated security systems designed to protect art collections from the thief and from such disasters as fire and water damage. It also contains some simple security suggestions for the collector, gallery, and institution. When applied diligently, in their respective spheres, these systems should at least help deter the pilferage of one of man's greatest gifts to himself—his art.

Figure 4. Landscape with Cottages by Harmensz Rembrandt van Rijn. Bequest of Miss Adeline Van Horne. Another of the eighteen stolen paintings—collectively valued at two million dollars.

Comments on Security Systems and Alarms

The reader should note that security systems are generally classified in two categories—perimeter and area or space control. Perimeter control would cover the openings of the museum, such as windows, skylights, and doors. Area or space control would cover the space within the museum.

The perimeter guards are the simplest, least expensive, and easiest to install. These devices may include step or pressure mats, foil, tape, and magnetic switches. They, in effect, provide an electric barrier against intrusion of the building's perimeter. CCTV (closed circuit television) may be used to surveil the exterior, as well as the interior, of the museum. Access through doors can be controlled by simple locks; electric strikes; magnetic locks; push-button, remote switches; card readers; special keys; electronic, digital combination locks; and even by fingerprint scanner systems.

Once inside the museum, protection is provided by the guard and, in many instances, by some truly sophisticated electronic transceiver (transmitter plus receiver) systems that are capable of vast area coverage or that can be restricted to the protection of a single art object. These systems would include ultrasonic detectors, capacitance alarms, audio detectors, microwave alarms, and photoelectric and CCTVs.

All of these intrusion reporters may be tied into central station systems, on or off the premises, which receive their emergency signals and act on them. Newly developed computer consoles are site-designed to handle a building's entire mechanical operation. This would include such categories as fire and security systems, energy management, voice communications, sprinkler valve monitoring, emergency power systems, and lights. As a result of emergency signals received by the console, instructions appear on the monitoring screen, listing names of persons to be notified and remedial steps to be taken to handle the particular emergency.

During closed hours, the museum, gallery, or library might choose to switch its security from the guard to the various electronic systems available and to have its electronic system monitored by an off-premise central station. This would mean that the operator of the monitor at the central station would be responsible for interpreting the emergency signals from the protected premises and taking appropriate action. Museums and other institutions considering such arrangements should be absolutely certain that the central station is located close enough to the museum to respond in sufficient time. Alternatively, the museum might decide to opt for a custom-designed, on-site system, fully automated and manned by its own personnel.

The devices described hereafter are available from various manufacturers. Some can be used to complement systems already functioning. Some are modest in price, while others are quite expensive. It is recommended that careful evaluation be given to each and every purchase, so that the best system will be obtained for the consumer's specific needs. (Note that many of the devices described are suitable for the gallery, library, or collector's home.) However, the problem doesn't end with selection. Competent installation, utilization, and servicing should be given as much consideration as the selection of the system itself.

Security systems, no matter how sophisticated, rely upon alarms of some sort. The security industry breaks down the alarm reporting devices into two general classifications—the local alarm and the remote alarm. The local alarm systems are those that report an intrusion on the protected premises by issuing a loud, blaring noise, usually through sirens, resonating horns, bells, or buzzers. (Figure 5.) The remote alarms report intrusions from the protected premise to a distant point where the intrusion is recorded and acted upon.

Most security experts would agree that the local alarm that makes the loudest, sustained noise is probably the most effective one. The local alarm can also be designed to activate lights instead of an audible alarm or combine both the audible alarm and lights. Whether the alarm indicators are heard and/or seen, they inform the intruder that he has been discovered and will hopefully stop him from carrying out the burglary. Ideally, the local alarm will alert neighbors, passersby, or a police patrol, who might deter the intruder or even apprehend him. Important too is the fact that the local alarm will warn the occupant of the premises that an intrusion has occurred.

In addition to the local alarms, practically all security systems must have a remote alarm signal to respond to an intrusion. This remote alarm is sent to a distant point where it is monitored and from where corrective action is directed. Examples of remote monitoring locations might be privately owned guard services, police stations, or perhaps the home of friends or key personnel. Remote alarm signals are usually carried by commercial telephone lines, either the customer's or a direct leased line.

The most popular remote alarm device is the telephone dialer, which operates from the customer's telephone lines. Telephone dialers are manufactured in two types—direct dialer and direct wire. In the direct-dialer type an intrusion results in telephone calls being made to preprogrammed numbers and messages from tape cartridges informing the called party of the emergency. In the direct-wire type the intrusion sets off an emergency signal to the remote reporting

Figure 5. Various types of local alarms. From left to right are (1) alarm horn; (2) alarm bell; (3) fire-alarm light; (4) alarm chime. Photograph courtesy of Honeywell, Inc.

point, where a red light tells the operator that an emergency exists.

When the telephone dialer systems first came on the market they were programmed into the local police station's main telephone number; but heavy volume would sometimes jam the main line. To meet this problem some police departments now assign a special number just to handle dialer service calls. Privately owned answering services and central stations also are available to handle traffic for dialer service systems.

Alarm systems play a vital role in the protection of our cultural heritage. They are not problem-free, however, and nuisance or false alarms are their single greatest drawback. Nuisance alarms may be caused by defects within the device itself or by faulty installation. Frequent nuisance alarms destroy the effectiveness of any alarm system. Police, neighbors, and security guards become discouraged with a system that has caused troublesome nuisance alarms. Understandably, their response time increases and, of course, the longer it takes to respond to an alarm, the greater the possibility the thief will succeed or the fire will destroy.

In fact, the frequency of nuisance or false alarms is becoming such an annoying problem that many communities have passed ordinances which prescribe fines against the owners of burglar alarms that have a history of false alarms. Apparently, most false alarms are caused by negligence on the part of the owner or are set off for reasons other than an actual intrusion. In 1978 the borough council of Westwood, New Jersey passed an ordinance stating that first offenders can be fined up to twenty-five dollars or given a warning; but a third false alarm during the period of a year brings a fine of seventy-five dollars and a fourth violation will result in a fine of one hundred and fifty dollars. Officials hope this action will result in a reduced rate of false alarms and a more vigorous response to all alarms. An additional part of the ordinance requires that anybody having an alarm system in Westwood must register it with the local police authorities.

Once again, the reader is urged to shop carefully for one designed to meet his particular needs and to employ a competent maintenance service to care for his equipment.

1.
Perimeter Protection Devices

In turning to a discussion of the devices which protect the exterior or perimeter of a building, the author has chosen to limit the number of systems to a manageable few. These devices, though they may differ in size and shape, are designed to protect the circumference of the building and are not primarily concerned with the protection of space or area.

Step Mats

One of the most popular perimeter protection devices is the rubber or plastic step mat in which contact surfaces are embedded. The contacts remain open so long as no weight is placed on the mat. The contacts close when a weight comes down on them, triggering an alarm.

Many galleries in New York City place step mats under their carpeting just inside the doorways to alert gallery personnel of an intrusion. The step mat is also used in a similar way by many libraries, galleries, historical sites, and museums during business hours to alert employees that somebody has violated a sensitive area of that building.

Another application of the step mat is its use in small strips on window sills, underneath door jambs, and staircases.

The step mat's construction, down to about ⅛-inch (3.2-cm) thick, makes it very easy to conceal under carpeting. The under-carpet, step-mat runners are about 30 inches (76.2 cm) wide and can be purchased in up to 50-foot (15.2-m) long rolls. (Figures 6 and 7.)

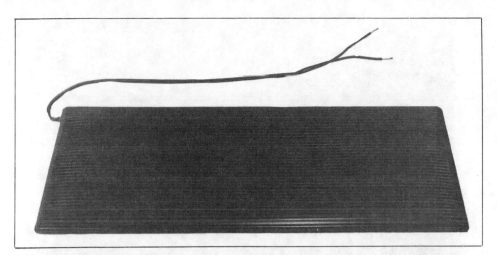

Figure 6. When a weight comes down on a rubber step mat an alarm is triggered. Photograph courtesy of Honeywell, Inc.

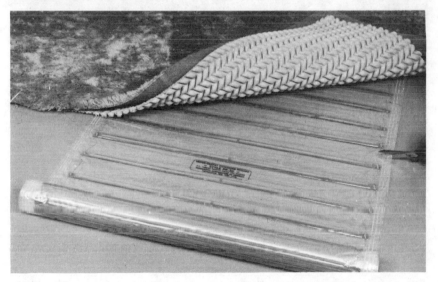

Figure 7. This type of step mat is easy to conceal under carpeting. The mat is only ⅛ inch thick. Photograph courtesy of Honeywell, Inc.

Magnetic Switches

This type of switch can be installed on any window or door. (Figure 8.) The switch itself has two pieces. One piece is a magnet and the other is a slide switch, which is furnished in an electrically closed setting. When the intruder opens the door or window, the magnet is moved away from the switch, which opens up, and an alarm is actuated.

Figure 8. This magnetic switch will set off an alarm if an intruder opens the door.

Wired, Wood-Dowelled Screens and Metallic Window Tape _____

To protect building areas that contain merchandise of high value, such as valuable art works stored in a warehouse, the walls and ceiling are covered by wired, wood-dowelled screens. These areas can be covered with wallboard for concealment purposes. Any attempt to penetrate these ceilings or walls will set off an alarm. Floors can be similarly treated by laying the floor over protective screening or wired panels.

Metallic window tape is of low ductility and tin-lead construction. When a window is broken or cracked, the current flowing through the tape is interrupted and an alarm is signalled. (Figures 9, 10, and 11.)

Figure 9. The walls and ceiling of this room have been covered with wired, wood-dowelled screens and the windows have been taped. If intruded upon, an alarm will be set off. Wallboard may be used to conceal the wired, wood-dowelled screens. Photograph courtesy of ADT.

Figure 10. The glass doors and transom of this typical modern retail store have been metallic-taped. Photograph courtesy of ADT.

Figure 11. A workman is applying metallic window tape as part of a building's perimeter protection alarm system. Photograph courtesy of ADT.

Closed Circuit Televisions

CCTV (closed circuit television) is a device often used to complement other security systems in a museum or art gallery. Many museums find CCTVs particularly effective for coverage of the remote areas of the museum, such as the loading and unloading docks, parking areas, windows, and certain doors.

Many companies offer CCTV cameras with costs ranging from less than three hundred dollars to more than five thousand dollars. After selection of the correct camera, as well as the console, the other factor to consider has been that a person usually is needed to monitor the system. However, the CCTV industry has now devised automatic monitoring devices which eliminate the need for a human observer. One of these devices is a photoelectric setup whereby photoelectric cells are attached to the monitoring television screen by ordinary rubber suction cups. These cells are organized so that they actually form a bridge circuit. The bridge circuit examines the level of light on the television monitoring screen. An intrusion of this picture causes the level of light to change within the photoelectric cells; the bridge circuit then becomes unbalanced and an alarm is activated.

The value of CCTV in helping deter crime was recently demonstrated by an unusual twist in the solving of a bank robbery. The August 6, 1977 edition of the *New York Daily News* carried an article headlined "Bank Gunmen Caught on TV."

Two gunmen wearing gloves and ski masks robbed the National Bank on Route 27 in Edison (N.J.) of $3,800 yesterday and escaped in a car driven by an accomplice.

Police said the bandits drove the tan and white auto to the American Can Co. plant off Plainfield Ave. in Edison where they switched cars.

The bandits didn't know it, but they were on TV when they tossed the bags of stolen cash from one vehicle to another, police said.

The crouching bank robbers were observed by an outdoor TV camera, part of plant security. An observant American Can Co. employee, watching the monitor indoors, noted the license plate number of the second getaway car and called police.

A New York City gallery, plagued by art thefts, has recently had CCTV installed. A camera was placed in each room of the gallery and the system was monitored by gallery personnel in a centrally located office. The manager of the gallery said the installation was not inexpensive. The CCTV probably paid for itself however, when two men recently tried to penetrate the inventory room during business hours and were thwarted in their attempt by the monitor operator, who dispatched a guard quickly to the scene.

Television is being used in many interesting ways to help solve art thefts. Donald Langton, the recently retired head of New Scotland Yard's Arts and Antiques Squad, is promoting the recording of art collections by the use of television tape. The art collector is featured on the tape, describing his art in detail. After the collection is recorded, the tape is presented to the collector with the recommendation that he keep it in a secure area, such as a safe-deposit box. If a theft should occur, the tape can be used as a ready source of identification when the victim files his theft report with the police and insurance authorities.

For the museum or gallery that is considering installing a CCTV surveillance program, considerable care must be taken in the selection of the equipment. The selection of the camera is critical, as without the correct camera there will not be a satisfactory image to monitor or record. If the camera is to be used twenty-four hours a day, with subdued lighting during the hours the museum is closed, then the camera selected should be a low-light-level type using the silicon target vidicon.

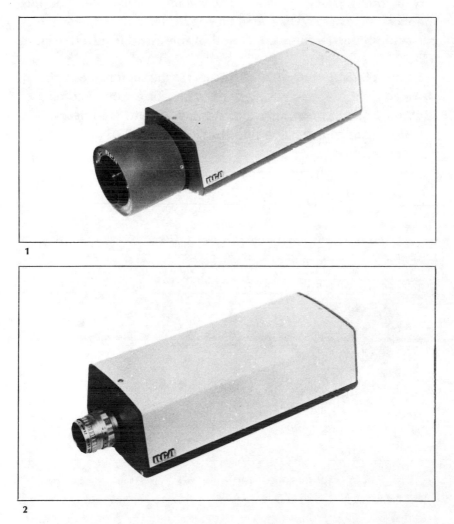

1

2

Figure 12. The two CCTV cameras shown in the photograph are (1) RCA's TC 1005/HO1 and (2) RCA's TC 1005/01. Photograph courtesy of RCA.

Some cameras operate well at high and low levels of light and an automatic iris lens should be installed on this camera to compensate for the varying light levels. (Figure 12.) The TC 1005/H01 is a low-light-level camera, using the silicon target vidicon. It has a picture resolution of seven hundred lines. The camera weighs 7.8 pounds (3.5 kg) without lens and in 1978 was priced at $1,250 without lens. The TC1005/01, using the standard antimony trisulfide vidicon, handles normal levels of light well. It has a picture resolution of eight hundred lines. Its list price for 1978 was $675 without lens.

While cameras are all important, additional equipment is necessary before a CCTV surveillance program is complete; housing, monitors, switchers, VTRs (video tape recorders), date/time generators and splitter/inserters are typical of the extras involved. (Figure 13.)

The Splitter/Inserter TC 1470 allows for the simultaneous display of video from two cameras on one monitor or for the recording of both on a single video tape recorder. The Splitter/Inserter weighs 2 pounds (0.5 kg) and its list price for 1978 was $285.

Figure 13. With RCA's TC 1470 Splitter/Inserter the video from two cameras can be shown on one monitor at the same time. Photograph courtesy of RCA.

Trip Wires

The trip wire device is usually installed across paths that an intruder might be likely to violate within a building. The trip wire is comprised of a spring, which is attached to a terminal block and a piece of wire with an end which fits into a ball-like fitting. When the intruder walks into the wire, he pulls the wire out of the ball-like fitting, opening the circuit and actuating the alarm. (Figure 14.)

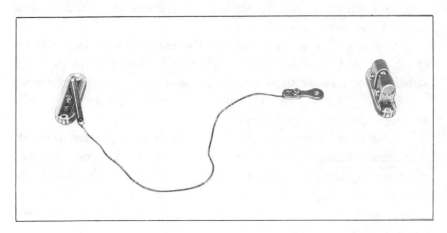

Figure 14. Trip wires are often placed across likely-to-be-crossed paths. When the intruder trips on the wire, he opens a circuit and sets off an alarm. Photograph courtesy of Honeywell, Inc.

Lighting

Good lighting on the exterior of a building has long been known as a deterrent to the burglar. The same can be said, perhaps, for an adequate lighting system within the building. The thief much prefers to work in the dark or in subdued light. The owner of the gallery and the administrator of the museum or library should check this defense periodically to assure that all of the facilities are adequately illuminated.

Parking lots, paths, doorways, fire escapes, windows, loading docks, emergency exit doors, and the corners of the building must be adequately lit to discourage the burglar. Lamps of 10 feet (3.0 m) or higher are often used and, generally speaking, the higher fixtures are more desirable. The vandal finds them more difficult to damage. It is also known that the effective ground-area coverage of an elevated lamp is usually about twice the height of the lamp. So, we can say that a 500-watt incandescent lamp rising 20 feet (6.1 m) off the ground can furnish adequate light for 40 feet (12.2 m) of a parking lot. There are a variety of high-intensity lights on the market that have the ability to illuminate large outdoor areas. Some of the lamps in sodium vapor or mercury vapor have bulb sizes up to 1,500 watts.

Stairwells, corridors, elevators, lobbies, and emergency exits are often neglected areas, as far as adequate lighting is concerned. The museum should solve this problem for protection against the thief, as well as for safety reasons. Low-wattage bulbs of 25 to 200 watts often suffice, and, if installed at close intervals, shadows and glare will be minimized.

Experience has determined that the exposed light bulb will be vandalized and, alternatively, that recessed lighting systems are more vandal-proof and accident-free. In general, lighting experts should be consulted to ensure that the gallery and museum have well-planned, functional lighting systems.

These brief comments on lighting, however important to building security, bring to mind the museum's even greater responsibility of protecting art from the harmful effects of light, both natural and artificial. The study of the effects of light upon art objects is a continuing one, and it is a very specialized and important area of conservation.

Madeleine Hours, chief curator of the French National Museums and manager of the research laboratory at the Louvre since 1945, recently wrote about the problems of light and art in a book called *Conservation and Scientific Analysis of Painting*. She observed:

> Paintings and other objects must be illuminated but in a
> controlled, measured way. Light sources can be natural,
> artificial or mixed. Natural lighting, coming from direct
> sunlight, is to be avoided. We know that protracted ex-
> posure to sunlight has thermal and photochemical effects
> that are as dangerous for humans as for paintings.

While she suggests constant vigilance concerning the effects of light on art, she also is pragmatic.

> There is no natural or artificial light source whose rays
> are altogether harmless, but that is no reason to keep
> works of art, that are made to be seen, in complete
> darkness.[2]

2. Madeleine Hours, *Conservation and Scientific Analysis of Painting* (New York: Van Nostrand Reinhold Company, 1976) 105–6.

2.

Interior Protection Devices

The systems designed to protect the interior of a building, though they report intrusions, as do the perimeter detectors, are primarily concerned with the coverage of vast space or area. There are many different types of space detectors, but, basically, their function is to record and report the motion of an intruder in the protected area. Also discussed here are access-control systems, such as locks and push-button access controls.

Locks

Much has been written about the highly sophisticated devices available today to protect our premises from the burglar. We speak of ultrasonic, infrared, microwave, and photoelectric security systems. However, we should not forget one of man's oldest deterrents to unwanted access—the lock.

While it is true that there is no such thing as an absolutely pick-proof lock, it is also true that if sufficient care is taken, a lock can accomplish a great deal. It actually can keep a thief out of the home, gallery, or museum.

Remember that we are fighting a delaying type of warfare against the burglar. The longer we can delay his access to the premises, the more chance we will have to discover his nefarious intentions and to thwart them. A good-quality, pick-resistant lock, used intelligently, can do much toward realizing this objective.

It is urged that the locking devices employed by the gallery, museum, or collector be reviewed by a competent locksmith. He may determine that your entire lock defense is outdated and too easily penetrable. Listen to his advice and consult him frequently about your lock problems. He should be available twenty-four hours a day. Your Chamber of Commerce or colleagues in the security field should be able to recommend a good locksmith. (Figure 15.)

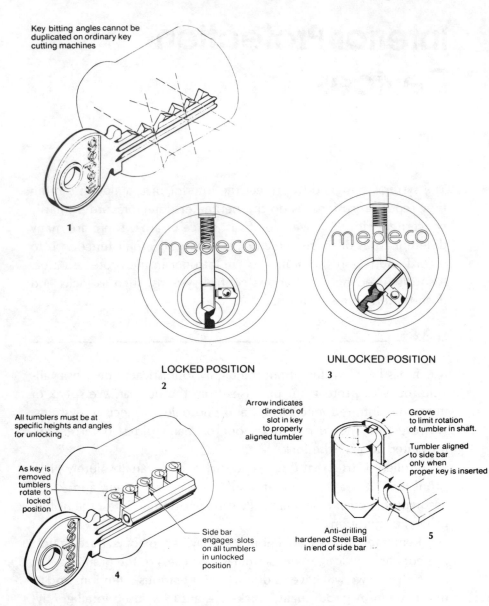

Figure 15.   The various features and components of a Medeco cylinder lock shown above are (1) the biting angles of a Medeco key; (2) locked position; (3) unlocked position; (4) tumbler positions are shown in locked and unlocked positions; (5) components of a Medeco cylinder. Photograph courtesy of Medeco.

Certain areas in museums, libraries, and some large art galleries are likely candidates for access-control. The entrance of an individual into such places as an inventory room, a confidential records center, private offices, security control areas, a room containing a safe and, in some instances, the building itself can be monitored in several ways.

One of the most popular access-control systems utilizes a plastic card similar in size to a credit card. The card is magnetically encoded. When inserted into a card reader by the user, the card reader interprets the code; if found to be valid, the door opens, permitting access. The card is lighter and easier to carry than keys and this system has become very popular. (Figure 16.)

A popular access-control system with built-in advantages is the digital access-control system, also referred to as the push-button combination door lock. The user pushes four or more buttons in a preset combination. When the correct combination of buttons is pushed, the door bolt retracts and permits access. (An example of this system is shown in Figures 17, 18, and 19.) It is called the Code/Tronic and its manufacturer, Sargent and Greenleaf, claims the selection of the combination "is as easy as selecting four numbers in the control panel." Changing the combination takes but a short time. The user can also adjust the door-latch control, including the amount of time he wants the door to remain unlocked, by making simple finger adjustments in the control panel.

This digital access unit, in various models, offers ten thousand to one million possible combinations. It can be hooked up to an alarm system, or a latch-inhibit feature will provide the capability to tie into a second system, which serves as an additional security step. For example, it can be tied into a guard-monitored television system. A latch time-reset unit cancels the unused latch-time as soon as the door closes, thus providing maximum security.

Prices for different models run from $360 to $633. The control box measures 11.5 inches (292 mm) in height and is 5.25 inches (133.4 mm) wide; it weighs 8 pounds (3.6 kg). The input panel weighs 3.25 pounds (1.5 kg), is 4.5 inches (114.3 mm) wide, 6 inches (152.6 mm) high, and 4 inches (101.6 mm) deep.

The push-button technique eliminates the use of a key or a card. There is nothing to carry, lose, or forget (except the combination).

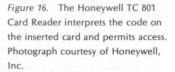

Figure 16. The Honeywell TC 801 Card Reader interprets the code on the inserted card and permits access. Photograph courtesy of Honeywell, Inc.

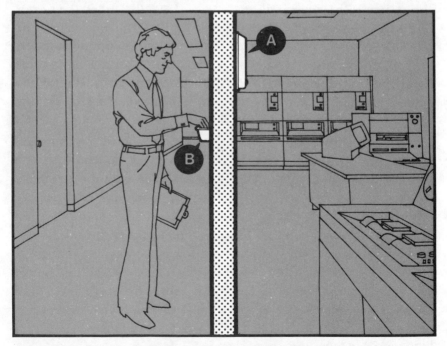

Figure 17. The Code/Tronic is a digital access-control system that permits access after the user has pushed the correct combination of buttons. The control panel (A) operates an electric door latch and is located within the secured area to prevent tampering. The input panel (B) is located in a hall or public area. Illustration courtesy of Sargent and Greenleaf, Inc.

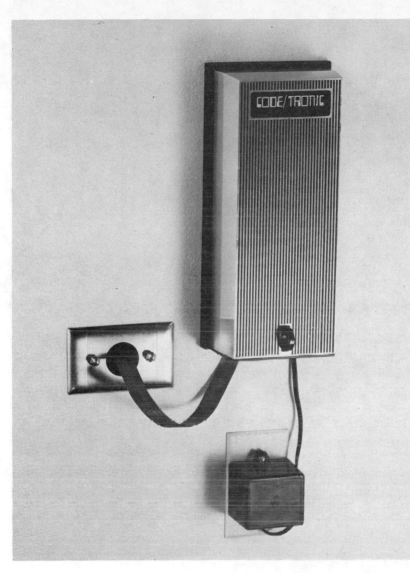

Figure 18. The control panel of the Code/Tronic. Photograph courtesy of Sargent and Greenleaf, Inc.

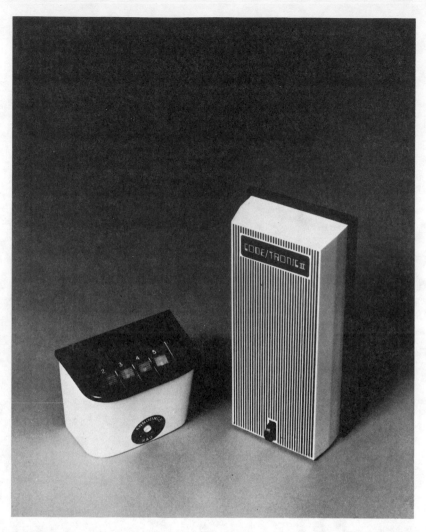

Figure 19. The input panel and the control panel of the Code/Tronic. Photograph courtesy of Sargent and Greenleaf, Inc.

However, the author believes that those who use the combination lock, push-button system should be conscientious about not revealing the combination to unauthorized individuals. Frequent changing of the combination is also recommended, particularly immediately after an employee resigns, retires, or is discharged.

One of the latest, and quite sophisticated, access-control systems is the Printrak 250D, manufactured by Rockwell International. The Printrak 250D permits access by identifying the user through his fingerprints. No two fingerprints are alike and, as the manufacturer points out, "unlike badges, keys, or cards, fingerprints can't be lost, stolen, or forgotten."

After entering an identification number into the Printrak 250D by pressing the correct keys on the system's ten-key keyboard, the user places a finger on a scanner. The system then compares the scanned fingerprint with the fingerprint on file and authorizes or denies access. This is an instrument of the future, and the author can easily see its potential for use by the large institution. The system, in addition to being used for access, also records activity. A printout informs the reader of the identity, time, and location of the individual gaining access.

Capacitance Alarms

Capacitance alarms set up an invisible RF (radio-frequency) field around a specific object or objects. The object itself acts as a part of the capacitance field and any disturbance or change in the area of the protected object, such as that caused by an intruder, causes a change in the capacitance. With the change in capacitance an imbalance occurs, which signals an alarm.

Capacitance alarms are generally used for the protection of a specific, valuable object, whether it be a painting, statue, safe, desk, a filing cabinet containing classified documents, or display and exhibit cases. Since the capacitance alarm is generally used to protect specific objects, the protective field of coverage is kept down to a specific depth, usually a few inches from the surface of the protected object, which must be ungrounded. The ability of the capacitance alarm to concentrate on small areas of coverage also means that this type of alarm can be used to protect art objects during business hours, as well as night hours when the gallery or museum may be closed.

The ADT Telapproach burglar alarm system is a capacitance-type alarm used frequently in museums and galleries to protect art works. The painting or paintings to be protected are mounted on copper-clad building paper, or they are foil-backed or foil-lined, connecting with the circuit in the capacitance unit so that its electrical capacitance-to-ground effect is part of a balanced RF circuit. The body capacitance of a person approaching the protected painting disturbs the electronic circuit, turning on a transistor and initiating an alarm in the associated control unit. (Figures 20, 21, and 22.)

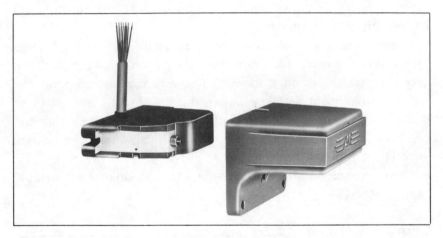

Figure 20. The ADT Telapproach unit and the housing for the system is a good example of a capacitance-type alarm for use in museums and galleries. Photograph courtesy of ADT.

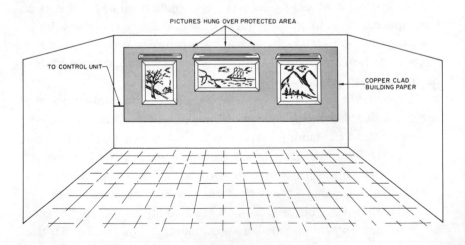

Figure 21. In the capacitance system paintings to be protected are mounted on copper-clad building paper. A person approaching will disturb the RF circuit and set off an alarm. Illustration courtesy of ADT.

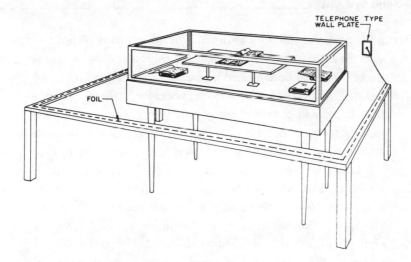

TELEPHONE TYPE
WALL PLATE

FOIL

Figure 22. The capacitance alarm system can also be used to protect rare books, coins, and other objects that are resting in an enclosed glass case. Illustration courtesy of ADT.

Infrared Systems

The use of infrared as an intrusion detector is a result of fairly recent technology. This system, which senses quick changes in infrared energy, has many advantages over other detection systems. First of all, it is not affected by noises, sound, air motion disturbances, or radio interference; it is a rather stable system. Secondly, materials such as glass, steel, concrete, and wood will block infrared energy. It will not penetrate walls or partitions. Infrared is often used to protect show windows and glass exhibit cases.

The infrared system is passive in nature, meaning that it does not require a signal to be transmitted. The optical system of the device defines the area being protected and any rapid change in the infrared energy in the area, caused by the body heat of an intruder, will trigger an alarm. The infrared system has a pattern of coverage which can accommodate a room approximately 30 by 30 feet (9.1 by 9.1 m). The pattern is omni-directional, wide, and fanlike in shape.

Problem areas for this system, which might cause nuisance alarms, are sunlight, animals, and radiators. Some of these problems can be solved by not aiming the sensor directly at the radiator or into the direct rays of the sun. The problem of animals can be solved by aiming the sensor a few feet above the floor, so that animals such as mice will pass under the covering pattern of the system.

Seismic Systems

Donald Langton comments about the seismic alarm system:

> You may not be aware of this, but a thief will enter a premise at the most convenient place to suit him. He will quite definitely not always use a door, window, skylight, or ventilator. He will consider going through a wall from an adjoining room or premises or an outside wall backing on to an alleyway. He might be disposed to the idea of entering a premise by coming up through a floor or going through a ceiling. But this is where the seismic alarm will provide adequate cover. The principle of this device is to detect vibration. The slightest movement in a wall, floor, or ceiling will activate the alarm. It can be modified to account for the movement of a mouse or the vibration caused either by underground railways or passing vehicles on the road.

A similar device to that described by Mr. Langton is the stress-change detector. These detectors are secured beneath floors, roofs, stairs, porches, or in any other area where an intruder walks. The stress-change detectors will note even very diminutive flexure of the area and will activate an alarm relay. Each detector can protect an area of about 300 square feet (27 sq m) and any number of detectors can be combined to afford coverage of a very large area.

This rather stable system is not affected by changes in temperature or sound and may be used indoors or out. Stress detectors will not work on materials having low flexure, such as cement, slate, cinder blocks, brick, or steel beams; and yet, an intruder's weight on a steel fire escape tread or on a wood or metal ladder rung will cause sufficient flexure of that material to activate an alarm.

Ultrasonic Systems

One of the most widely used electronic security systems in museums and galleries is the type referred to as ultrasonic (sound inaudible to the human ear). The ultrasonic system works on the principle of the Doppler effect, which states that any pertinent movement between a source of sound and a receiver causes a shift in the frequency. The system interprets this shift as an intrusion.

The ultrasonic system detects all forms of motion within the targeted area. Since the ultrasonic field is invisible, it is difficult for the criminal to detect or fool it. To be truly effective, though, the ultrasonic system should be installed in an environment which is free of such troublesome factors as high level noises, air currents, moving machinery, building vibrations, chandeliers, venetian blinds, and animals. Failure to consider these factors when installing an ultrasonic device will result in excessive amounts of nuisance alarms.

The effective range of the ultrasonic pattern of coverage is approximately 30 feet (9.1 m) and the pattern is omni-directional. The gallery or museum that has an ultrasonic system installed may find it necessary to call the service company periodically regarding nuisance-type alarms. The serviceman will try to rectify the condition by tuning down the system. The danger here, though, is that the tuning-down process may reduce the effectiveness of the individual unit's pattern of coverage to a few feet; and, since the area of installation is often in a ceiling or on a part of the wall close to the ceiling, the designated area of protection may not be receiving any coverage. This potential problem should be brought to the serviceman's attention and frequent checks should be made to assure proper coverage.

Figure 23. Ultrasonic systems, such as the Ademco Ultra Ultrasonic 450, are based on the Doppler effect—a significant motion between the source of sound and the receiver will cause a frequency shift. Photograph courtesy of Ademco.

The total area of coverage for the ultrasonic system can be greatly expanded by adding as many as twenty transceivers, all functioning on but a single amplifier. Therefore, if a single transceiver has an area of coverage measuring 20 by 30 feet (6.1 by 9.1 m) in an oval pattern, twenty transceivers would increase the coverage to 400 by 600 feet (122 by 183 m). (Figure 23.) The unit shown in the photograph is advertised as having adjustable transducer heads, which permit selective area protection. The Turbulence Warning System helps the installer by constantly checking the air for air currents and turbulence, helping to avoid potential trouble areas. The system also features a Doppler Discriminator and specially designed electronic filters that protect against nuisance alarms caused by radio interference or hissing radiators. The measurements of this ultrasonic device are 10½ by 4½ by 2 inches (25.7 by 11.4 by 5.1 cm).

Photoelectric Systems (Electric Eye)

The photoelectric intrusion system is frequently used to complement other types of intrusion devices. It can furnish vital protection of a building's walls or ceilings and can also be used to cover long rows of windows (like those typically found in museums). Some photoelectric units that use infrared beams will afford coverage up to 1,000 feet (305 m).

The principle involved here is the breaking of a beam of light between a projector and a receiver (sensitive to light) located at a considerable distance away. Once the beam is broken, as by an intruder, an alarm is actuated. A major disadvantage of this system is that the light beam is visible. However, infrared beams, which cannot be seen, are available and should be utilized.

Some of these systems use mirrors to provide premises protection in a crisscross pattern. Considerable care should be taken during the installation to conceal the projector, receiver, and mirrors. Concealment is important in two ways: firstly, to hide the system from the intruder, and, secondly, to protect the units from being bumped or moved, which causes misalignment and malfunction of the system. (Figure 24.) The manufacturer claims this system has a 350-foot (107-m) beam, is UL listed for central station and local alarm use, and has a fully concealed alignment system to provide 180-degree horizontal and 10-degree vertical adjustment. The unit also has rechargeable, standby batteries built into the transmitter and receiver to provide twelve-hour emergency power during AC power failure. It measures 3¼ inches in width and is 5 inches in height and 2¼ inches in depth (8 by 13 by 6 cm).

Figure 24. With photoelectric systems, such as the Ademco 1325 Photoelectric System, an invisible beam of light is projected. When an intruder intercepts the beam, an alarm is sounded. Photograph courtesy of Ademco.

Microwave Alarms

Microwave alarm systems issue an RF greater than ten million hertz (cycles per second) and constantly measure the microwave energy field bouncing back from surrounding surfaces. The RF used by this system are those at least 100 thousand times greater than those shown on the dial of your kitchen radio. When the microwave field of energy is disturbed, as by a moving person, the RF waves are returned at a frequency different than the one at which they were transmitted. This difference registers as a low-frequency signal and an alarm is sounded.

The microwave system, which operates on the Doppler principle, has many attractive qualities, two of which are:

1. It is not influenced by air currents, light, noise, humidity or temperature changes.

2. It has an effective range that exceeds many security systems.

In fact, if the coverage pattern is extended by using a long narrow pattern, the effective range can be pushed up to about 300 feet (91 m). This pattern might be ideal in a building with long, narrow corridors similar to those found in museums and libraries. The protective pattern can be reduced in length and made wider with an effective range of from 75 to 100 feet (23 to 30 m).

Microwaves penetrate walls and partitions, particularly those made of wood and glass. Metals, such as steel, reflect microwaves, as do floors made of concrete. This means that proper installation is essential to avoid nuisance alarms triggered by outside factors, such as radar signals or moving objects. Advantageously, it also means that this system can be installed in a closet or some similar hidden area and still maintain a respectable degree of efficiency.

In microwave systems nuisance-type alarms can be actuated by moving chandeliers, venetian blinds, and fluorescent lights; and, while the microwave system can be applied outdoors, animals, especially birds, make this type of program rather impractical for any other than fenced-in areas. (Figure 25.) The manufacturer claims that the unit shown in the photograph has been developed to filter out electrical "noise," which has always been the source of nuisance alarms in microwave detectors, particularly those caused by power lines and fluorescent lighting. For best results the microwave detector should be installed at least 3 feet (.9 m) away from the fluorescent lights.

This unit offers wide-angle, 150-degree coverage, and it is available in four operating frequencies. Thus, up to four detectors or

Figure 25. When the microwave field of energy is disturbed a microwave detector, such as the Ademco 360, will pick up the disturbance and sound an alarm. Photograph courtesy of Ademco.

transceivers (transmitter plus receiver) can protect a single area without mutual interference or "cross talk" occurring between the units.

Power for this transceiver is supplied directly from a low-voltage, plug-in transformer, which maintains a constant charge on a 12-volt rechargeable battery in the power supply. In the event of a power failure, up to twelve hours of reserve power is available for one transceiver and six hours for two transceivers.

Audio-Detection Systems

This particular intrusion detector operates on the sound or audio-detection principle. It does not work on the Doppler principle, but rather it employs a series of microphones located in the secured building.

Institutions that have public-address systems can easily convert to an audio-detection program by coupling to the already installed microphones. These detectors listen to the sounds emanating from the various rooms in which the microphones are located; if an intrusion occurs, an alarm will be signalled. The operator of the central station console, whether located on the secured premises or off, can actually hear what is taking place in the designated rooms and will be in a position to alert the guards and/or police if an intrusion has been indicated. An additional feature of this system is that when the alarm is sounded at the central station a tape is activated to record what has been heard. This recording may prove useful as evidence in any future court proceeding.

The March 19, 1977 edition of the New York Times, carried a story on an audio-detection system developed by Sonitrol Security System.

The microphones, which have an effective range of 8,000 square feet in a hard-surface room—one without carpets, drapes or other sound-absorbing materials—are hooked into leased telephone lines to the local Sonitrol office.

The sensitivity of the microphones was demonstrated one Sunday morning several weeks ago, when a Sonitrol operator in Hartford picked up sounds of dripping water in the gallery of the Connecticut State Library. The police response was credited with preventing extensive damage to portraits and other artifacts.

Silent Alarms

Art museums, galleries, and libraries should also consider installing silent alarm devices to protect their personnel from the armed robber or crazed individual. (Figure 26.) Some types of silent alarms can be sounded by pulling a button. According to the manufacturers, the button is pulled, rather than pressed, so that no telltale muscular movement can be observed in the upper arm. The silent alarm unit may be connected to a central station, directly to local police headquarters, or to a proprietary or local alarm service. This is a small device, measuring $5\tfrac{15}{16}$ inches in length, $1\tfrac{7}{8}$ inches wide, and $\tfrac{7}{8}$ inch deep (15.0 by 4.7 by 2.2 cm).

Figure 26. This hand-operated silent alarm can be mounted in any convenient, concealed location, such as behind a desk. Photograph courtesy of ADT.

A Fully Secured Premise

Pictured in Figure 27 is what one manufacturer calls a "fully secured premise." Shown are ultrasonic and photoelectric systems, foil and window contacts, and the facility that will allow alarms to be received at a central station and/or police headquarters. Also shown are trap door and cabinet protection.

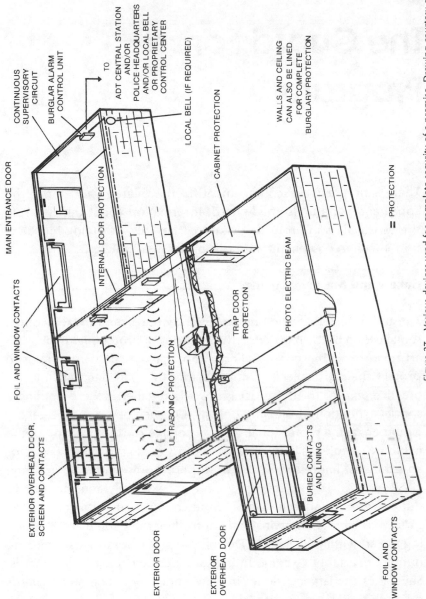

CONTINUOUS SUPERVISORY CIRCUIT

BURGLAR ALARM CONTROL UNIT

MAIN ENTRANCE DOOR

TO

ADT CENTRAL STATION
AND/OR
POLICE HEADQUARTERS
AND/OR LOCAL BELL
OR PROPRIETARY
CONTROL CENTER

LOCAL BELL (IF REQUIRED)

INTERNAL DOOR PROTECTION

CABINET PROTECTION

WALLS AND CEILING
CAN ALSO BE LINED
FOR COMPLETE
BURGLARY PROTECTION

FOIL AND WINDOW CONTACTS

TRAP DOOR PROTECTION

PHOTO ELECTRIC BEAM

= PROTECTION

EXTERIOR OVERHEAD DOOR, SCREEN AND CONTACTS

ULTRASONIC PROTECTION

EXTERIOR DOOR

EXTERIOR OVERHEAD DOOR

BURIED CONTACTS AND LINING

FOIL AND WINDOW CONTACTS

Figure 27 Various devices used for complete security of a premise. Drawing courtesy of ADT.

43

3.
The Guard Force Program

There is no greater discouragement for the thief or vandal than the appearance of a uniformed guard. Information about the vital role the guard plays in protecting our art treasures, including his selection, training, equipment, and responsibilities, follows.

Gallery and Museum Guards

The author feels that a well-trained guard force of men and/or women remains one of the most effective methods of protecting the world's art treasures in museums. Galleries too, may certainly use guards to protect their art objects. Until recently this had been an unusual practice, except for those occasions when galleries were holding a special exhibition of valuable objects. On such occasions the gallery would engage a professional security service for the duration of the exhibit. Knoedler Gallery in New York City engaged such a service for an exhibit of impressionist and postimpressionist paintings from the USSR in 1973. The exhibit drew large crowds daily and the guards' duties were extended to handling the crowds waiting to get into the gallery, as well as observing and controlling the people and protecting the art within the gallery. During the past several years, while the number of art thefts was mounting, galleries began to employ guards. Several of the larger galleries in New York City now employ guards on a full-time basis. (Figure 28.)

Figure 28. As the number of art thefts increases, more and more museums and galleries are hiring guards on a full- or part-time basis. Photograph courtesy of ADT.

A survey by the author of ten United States museums brought forth some interesting facts about their guard forces:

1. None of the museums surveyed were manned by outside, private guard forces. The museum administrators appear to have concluded that it is more effective to hire and train their own guards.

2. The use of the outside guard force seemed to be limited to occasions when extra personnel were needed to supplement the regular force, such as for a popular exhibition. Some museum guards commented that even on these occasions the outside agencies often dispatched different men to the museum each day, thus necessitating a daily explanation of the responsibilities. The regular museum guard is also disturbed by the fact that the outside guard's remuneration is usually greater than his.

(The advantages of hiring an outside guard force, however, should be considered: The outside agency relieves the museum of the burden of interviewing, screening, hiring, and training of personnel; they handle union matters between management and labor; they are responsible for supplying and maintaining any equipment the guard force needs, including uniforms; and they are also responsible for supplying additional personnel when illness and vacations occur.)

3. Museum guards, because of their low pay-scale, usually are drawn from two distinct groups—the college student attempting to supplement his parent's contributions and the retired person attempting to supplement his pension. Turnover is high because of poor pay and the fact that the job is often monotonous. The survey indicated that the young college student is the least reliable and that the female is more reliable than the male in this group. The retired man, on the other hand, finds the low salary easier to handle and was judged to be the most reliable employee in the guard force.

(Actually, there is a third category of guards—the city employee. The director of security of a large midwestern museum stated that all of the people involved in the maintenance of the museum building, including the guard force, are city employees. He has no voice in the selection of personnel; they are sent to him by city hall. They have had no training in museum work and, furthermore, have little or no interest in the museum or in art. The situation is further complicated by the fact that many of these employees received their jobs as a result of the political patronage system. They are very open about their alleged "influence" with the mayor's office and their immediate supervisors often find them to be difficult employees.)

4. Two museums recently were able to obtain a pay hike for their guards and have started to attract a middle group. A large portion of this group consists of women, many of whom are divorced or who feel their children no longer need them during the school day.

5. There is a definite trend away from the traditional guard uniform, which resembled that of a police officer. Often museums dress their guards in sport jackets and slacks. This is a commendable development, providing that the attire is quite distinctive and easily identifiable by the public. A nameplate on the jacket is desirable.

6. Only one of the ten museums surveyed employed guards who were armed at all times. Many museum administrators feel that when dealing with the large crowds museums are drawing today firearms are potentially too dangerous. They are especially fearful that innocent people might be injured or killed in an emergency situation. Some have also said that patrons often are "turned off" by the display of so much authority. Others feel that it might be agreeable for the guards to wear firearms during the hours when the museum is closed.

If the museum does permit its security force to carry firearms, then it must assure that the equipment issued is in excellent working condition and that the training program includes instruction in the use and maintenance of firearms. An initial course in firearms training is not sufficient. The correct training program should include firing the revolver at a supervised range on a monthly basis and should extend throughout the guard's employment.

Hiring and Training the Guard

Whether the museum decides to hire an outside guard agency or develop a guard force within the museum, an adequate training program must be insisted upon if the guard force is to be effective.

Each museum should employ one person as the director of security. In addition to supervising the activities of the guard force, the director should have a voice in the selection of his personnel. He should have direct responsibility for training the guard force. When an opening occurs in the guard force the director should sit in on the interviews of applicants.

Each institution should insist that all of its employees be finger-printed. The applicant should not be hired until the results of the fingerprint examination are known. Failure to adhere to this principle can lead to tragic results.

The May 19, 1977 *New York Daily News* printed an article called "State Isn't Guarding Guard Business," which reported that in New York State:

> Slipshod screening procedures and weak state laws are allowing persons accused—and sometimes convicted—of crimes to operate security guard firms or work for them as guards. Their crimes varied but included arson, theft, assault, extortion, and child abuse. One guard employed by a private guard service, threw an eight-year-old boy to his death from a rooftop. The guard firm had not submitted his fingerprints to the Department of State in Albany, New York, within twenty-four hours after he was hired, as required by law. Had the fingerprint check been conducted, investigators said, the firm would have learned that the guard . . . had a record of four convictions, including one for sexually abusing a child."

The International Association of Chiefs of Police, "Police Executive Report," dated April 29, 1977, carried an article called "Private Security Guards Need More Training." It said that a recent report prepared by the Task Force on Private Security, funded by the Law Enforcement Assistance Administration, had recommended "that all private watchmen, guards, and detectives be required to register with the state and that private security businesses be required to obtain state licenses."

All guard personnel should receive instruction in their training programs on how to respond to emergency situations in the museum, such as fire, bursting pipes, theft, vandalism, power shortages, crowd control, and illness. Each museum should have a plan of action and the plan should be reviewed frequently to remain effective.

The Guard Force Art Inventory Sheet

The security director of a large museum recently admitted that on one occasion his staff had not confirmed that an art object was actually missing for several shifts; this, in spite of the fact that several guards had noticed the object was missing from its normal location.

When asked if the guard force used the art inventory system to verify the location of the art exhibited on each shift the director said they wouldn't have had time to do such a thing.

This is an unacceptable explanation. The use of the inventory sheet is essential to good security. Each guard should have a typed list of the art objects for which he is responsible. The list should be kept current and should be small enough to keep in the guard's book of regulations or in some other easily accessible place. The inventory sheet should be checked before and after the guard's shift. During his shift, an alert guard should be constantly scanning the art pieces for which he is responsible. The director of security should be responsible for noting any change on the art inventory sheet and for notifying his personnel of the change. He, in turn, should be notified by the respective curator of any contemplated changes.

Several security directors have stated that their museums do not have a firm policy on this subject. Several department heads have ignored requests by security personnel to advise them beforehand about changes in the exhibited inventory. Their failure to do this causes anxious moments for the security staff, who ultimately are burdened with the responsibility of tracking down the missing object in the museum. Failure to advise the guard force that certain objects have been removed from an exhibit by museum personnel for routine reasons is inexcusable, and museum administrators should see to it that this shortcoming is eliminated.

Guard Duty During Secured Hours

The security director of a large midwestern museum has stated that his museum, like most museums, employs only a minimal force when the museum closes for the day. He feels much more comfortable about the security of the museum at night than during the day, pointing out that even he cannot get into the museum at night unless he makes an official request in advance.

He stated that the main access areas to the museum during secured hours receive electronic protection and guard coverage. The more inaccessible areas are very well lighted and receive electronic coverage. Additionally, the local police provide patrol car coverage to the exterior of the museum. He is constantly reminding his guard force about the different ploys a criminal might use to gain access to the museum at night.

A large museum in Massachusetts fell victim to a ruse several years ago. A man left a package in the museum saying he would call for it "later." "Later" turned out to be after the museum had closed. The man said he had returned for his package. The guard opened the door and found himself looking down the barrel of a revolver. The gunman and some companions rushed into the museum and made off with a Greco-Roman rare coin collection valued at over two million dollars.

Guard Dogs

A beautiful west coast museum has added guard dogs to its security system. The dogs are used in the museum at night and, according to the security director, have worked out so well that a human guard has been dropped from the night shift. The dogs, who happen to be German shepherds, were obtained from a nearby kennel and are returned to the kennel periodically for a refresher course.

The dogs work with more than one handler efficiently. Normally, a dog stays with the handler during museum rounds, but it can be turned loose to check the rooms ahead of time and does so with speed and thoroughness. The dog's superior sense of smell enables him to find any intruder with dispatch. The dogs have not presented a sanitation problem and will "tell" the handler when it is time to go "out." Many trainers recommend female dogs for this duty. Females do not lift their legs when urinating and, therefore, are not as likely to stain the base of a statue should an accident occur.

At a recent police convention, there were several guard-dog booths. One posted a bulletin listing the advantages of using a dog for guard duty. In essence, they included such statements as:

1. He doesn't chase women or drink alcoholic beverages on duty.
2. He doesn't call in sick.
3. He doesn't take any vacations or holidays.
4. He doesn't belong to any union, nor does he go on strike.
5. He doesn't have a salary.

However, the disadvantages of using dogs might occur when the handler becomes ill or moves on to other employment, or if the dog has to be replaced. (Figure 29.)

Figure 29. There are many advantages to using guard dogs. This particular German shepherd is named Linzmeyer Choice of Troymara C.D. Photographed by Pat Spear.

The Guard's Equipment

Many museums have telephone stations located near the post where the guard is on duty. The guard can use this phone to check in with the man on duty in the museum's security room, to ask for relief, or to alert the security room of a theft or an act of vandalism. In many museums this telephone service is the only electronic communication system available to the guard. It is good equipment, but it is not portable.

Every museum guard should be issued a freshly charged two-way portable FM radio at the beginning of each shift. At the end of each shift, the guard should place the radio in the battery-charger rack, which is usually located in the security room of the museum. The use of the two-way portable radio allows the guard a method of relaying emergency-type information to his base station, which also is usually located in the security room. He can also relay the same type of information to his fellow officers. One can easily see the value of such equipment during the pursuit of a thief, but the time such a system might save in reporting the sudden illness of a guard or patron, or the reporting of a fire, is just as apparent.

Unnecessary voice traffic should be forbidden so that the air waves are free to handle emergency transmissions. As is the case with all equipment, the guard should receive training in the use and care of the portable radio. Many of the companies that sell this product have representatives that will give such instruction upon request. The security director or his designate should keep a constant inventory of the portable radio equipment to be certain it is functioning and is being used properly. He should also maintain a daily log, indicating who used the equipment and when it was used. Loss or theft of this equipment should be reported immediately to the security director. The guard should realize that two-way portable FM radios are expensive. They usually sell for more than one thousand dollars each. (Figure 30.)

The portable radio shown also has attached an optional external microphone, which permits the operator to use the radio without removing it from its holder. This radio can be obtained in any of six different housing sizes and is designed to provide up to eight frequencies. The sizes and weights of the radios in this series are variable due to the choice of radio housing sizes and battery combinations. The series offers eight different batteries in six sizes, permitting flexibility in choice of duty cycles, charge rates, and hours of operation. All batteries have a twist-off connector, which allows removal and installation in seconds.

Some museums are now using personal one-way paging devices to keep in touch with their key personnel. An operator using a paging terminal or manual encoder and a series of transmitters is able to send a message tone to the individual wearing the paging receiver. The message tone is usually in the form of a constant beep, but some systems are capable of sending a message tone in the form of a vibration. When the message tone is received, the party can then obtain his message by telephoning his office. Some paging systems permit the sender to give the receiver the message by voice.

As in the case of two-way portable FM radios, the pagers use batteries; and, yes, they too must be recharged periodically! (Figure 31.)

The pager shown in the photograph weighs only 4.5 ounces (127.6 g) and its sensitive receiver assures positive personal contact within the system coverage area—office, plant, car, or home. It has a variable volume control and is available in either highband VHF (very-high frequency) or UHF (ultra-high frequency). Furthermore, the unit provides the correct audio level for almost any environment you enter. An optional lapel speaker can be plugged into the external speaker jack to bring the alert tone and voice message right up to the ear in high noise areas. Another feature is Mem-O-Lert deferred paging, which enables the user to defer the audio-alerting signal. Received paging signals are silently stored until the user has the opportunity to request them.

Both the two-way portable FM radio's and paging system's traffic can be handled by the central station on or off the premises, or by the latest fully automated, on-site security and building-management consoles.

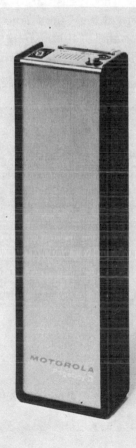

Figure 30. An important part of the museum's guard equipment is a freshly charged two-way FM radio. The one shown here is a Motorola Handie-Talkie, MX300 Series. Photograph courtesy of Motorola.

Figure 31. The Motorola Pageboy II radio pager can be carried in a shirt pocket or clipped to a belt. Photograph courtesy of Motorola.

During the closed hours of the museum, guards proceed to protect the building and its contents in an organized procedure called a "tour." The program is organized to ensure that a tour is started and completed in a predetermined time and to protect the guard while he is on tour.

An alarm signal, known as an "exception alarm," is initiated only if a tour is not completed in sequence within the time period programmed. This eliminates the constant monitoring of other systems. Instead of receiving all tour signals, the central station will only receive signals when the guard fails to complete a tour on time.

The Wells Fargo WTS-3 Watchman Tour System, recently renamed the Guard Tour System, is a typical tour program. The components of this system are the tour control, charger, key, and active and passive stations. (Figure 32.)

Figure 32. A tour system control program is used as a back-up system for the museum guard. An alarm signal is triggered if the guard does not complete the tour sequence in the time allotted. The system shown here is the Wells Fargo WTS-3 Watchman Tour System renamed the Guard Tour System. Photograph courtesy of Wells Fargo.

Figure 33. The tour control, shown here in its case, is one of the components of the Guard Tour System. Photograph courtesy of Wells Fargo.

The tour control (shown in its case in a closed position in Figure 33) is the central control for the tour system. Its programmable tour-timing cycle is the core of the exception-reporting concept. It can be connected to fire-transmitting equipment and has a forty-station capacity that can be expanded to eighty stations by using a second control.

The charger (Figure 34) is a versatile support unit. It charges and tests the key battery and can also be used for system on/off control. The charger initiates a monitoring signal whenever it is used and resets the key sequence. The tour key (Figure 34) is inserted into stations in programmed sequence and is done on time to prevent exception-alarm signals from being sent. Green LED (light-emitting diodes) indicates a proper sequence, red LED indicates an incorrect sequence.

A maximum of four active stations (Figure 34) can be wired to one control. They provide the timing for the tour and can only be keyed during the last five minutes of the timing cycle. Failure to key a station will cause an alarm. Up to nine passive stations (Figure 34) can be installed for each active station installed. The passive stations require no wiring. Each passive station is programmed for a specific sequence in the tour and must be keyed in that order. The tour (Figure 35) could be programmed either as a single group of sixteen, groups of eight, or groups of four.

The Watchman Tour System (WTS-3) pictured operates in the following manner: test the key battery and reset sequence by depressing the Watchman Tour System push button. If the green indicator lights up, remove the key and begin the tour. If the charging station is used as the on/off control for the system, a start-tour signal will be initiated when the key is removed, and time-out will begin for the first tour segment. If an on/off switch is used, the starting signal will occur and time-out will commence when the on/off switch is turned to "on." The watchman proceeds to the first passive station in the first tour segment, and keys each and every station in the designated sequence until he reaches the active station at the end of the tour segment. He then waits for open timing window indicators

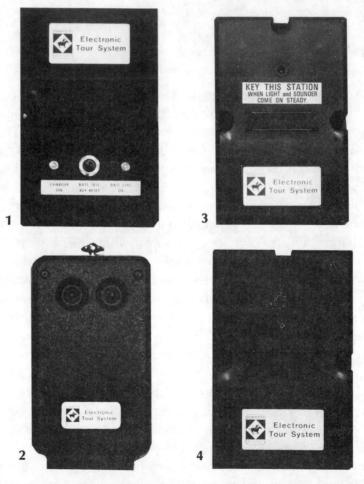

Figure 34. Components of the tour system from left to right are (1) the charger; (2) the tour key; (3) the active station; (4) the passive station. Photograph courtesy of Wells Fargo.

to be activated, and keys the active station before the timing window indicators go out. He then proceeds to the next station in the sequence and completes the next segment in the same manner, until the entire tour is completed.

When the tour is completed, the WTS-3 automatically cycles to the beginning of the tour, and begins the timing of the first tour segment. The watchman then repeats the tour on his assigned time schedule.

The WTS-3 is connected to a central station, usually located on the premises, which monitors the electronic signals of the tour. The central station will receive a start-tour signal and an end-tour signal when the system is turned on and off. All other signals are exception alarms and should be responded to as to an alarm.

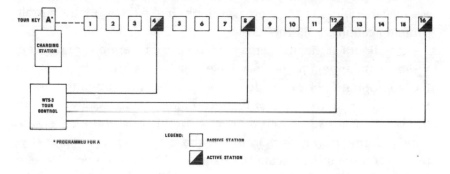

Figure 35. The Grand Tour, a typical guard's tour using the Wells Fargo WTS-3. Drawing courtesy of Wells Fargo.

Guides and Other Personnel

Many of the museums and galleries in the United States and abroad are located in buildings that originally were not built for this purpose. A visit to such buildings sensitizes one to the problems that the administration must attempt to resolve. Narrow passageways, narrow doors, blind areas caused by unneeded walls or partitions, undersized elevators that accommodate too few people, staircases and other building materials that may not have a respectable ability to resist fire; all create specific problems for the security of art and the safety of employees and visitors.

For museums or galleries yet to be constructed these are the problems to which an architect should address himself. Galleries can be designed so that visitor traffic can flow freely; there should be no "blind areas," where the sneak thief can operate. Attractive directional signs can be posted so that the visitor can feel secure in his movements; and to prevent unwanted wanderings into private or emergency areas of the museum, these private areas should be kept removed from the exhibits.

For the museum or gallery with traffic-flow problems one of the most desirable methods of maintaining steady traffic flow is to place a guide in the vicinity of the main entrance to the museum. He will answer questions about the building and its contents. Many of the large museums, such as the Metropolitan Museum of Art in New York City and the Field Museum of Natural History in Chicago, have information booths located near the main entrance. The personnel in these booths provide the visitor with directions to requested exhibit areas. Detailed floor plans are also available there and serve as excellent guides to these areas. Telephones in these booths permit communication within the museum.

The booth at the main area may serve as a reception area as well. Visitors with appointments may have a call made from the booth to the appropriate person or department. After the appointment has been confirmed, the clerk at the information booth issues a pass to the visitor. The pass should designate the identity of the caller, the date and time of the visit, and what the caller was carrying, if anything. It should also indicate the name of the museum employee to be seen. Some institutions permit the visitor to find his way to the office or department he is seeking, but, perhaps the visitor should be called for by a secretary or the person to be visited and guided to the appropriate meeting place. There should be a hard and fast rule that the visitor, no matter how special he may be, should not be permitted to wander throughout the museum without constant supervision by museum personnel. Without proper supervision, these visitors present mind-boggling potential for theft or vandalism. Upon completion of the visit, the museum employee should countersign the pass and show the caller out of the museum. The employee should then deposit the pass in a designated place. The museum should have a central repository for the passes where they can be filed daily. These passes can later prove to be invaluable should a theft, vandalism, or other type of incident occur. The pass system protects the interests of the museum, but just as importantly, it also may protect the visitor from being falsely charged with a crime.

4.
Security Against Fire

Burglary is not the only problem facing those concerned with the protection of works of art. Fire is a major threat. The security director of a Chicago museum has stated that he is far more concerned about fire than he is about theft; while theft is serious, fire can destroy a museum.

Just throughout the course of their normal day-to-day functions, museums are subject to numerous fire hazards. Renovation or the preparations for new exhibitions introduce such hazards as electrical wiring and temporary materials such as paints and solvents, soldering irons, and welding equipment. Fires can also start as a result of problems in the museum's heating equipment or kitchen facilities and through sloppy housekeeping and vandalism. Smoking always represents a threat and should only be permitted in restricted areas. Ask your fire department to designate areas where smoking may safely be permitted in your building. Many galleries in the United States and in Europe now post signs requesting the public not to smoke.

Many people seem to believe that museums are so well constructed that fire is no real threat. This statement couldn't be farther from the truth. Many museums are housed in buildings that were not originally designed for that purpose, such as old wooden churches. But, even where the museum is built of concrete and steel, fire can be devastatingly destructive, as the officials of the Museum of Modern Art in Rio de Janeiro, Brazil learned recently. On July 10, 1978, the *New York Times* reported in an article headlined, "Most Art Destroyed in Rio Fire" that:

Restoration experts at the fire-blackened Museum of Modern Art said today that they may be able to salvage only 50 of about 1,000 works of art damaged or destroyed yesterday in a flash fire that turned two exhibition halls into smoking piles of ash in 30 minutes. . . .

Fire officials said they believed the blaze began in a small theatre-auditorium on the top floor of the two-story, cantilevered, concrete and steel building. . . .

They said either an electrical short circuit or possibly a cigarette smoldering in upholstery kindled a slow fire that probably started to spread shortly after a concert ended at midnight Friday.

According to the National Fire Protection Association, fires develop in four stages:

1. In the incipient stage there is no visible evidence of fire. However, a chemical change or thermal decomposition of an object is occurring. This thermal decomposition produces airborne particles, which are not visible to the human eye. These particles act like a gas and rise to the building's ceiling. This stage is slow in development and can last anywhere from a few minutes to several days.

2. In the next stage smoke is evident. Smoke, which can take lives, is followed by flames in minutes. Art works that suffer smoke damage can often be restored.

3. In this stage flames break out and the fire is on its way to destroying almost anything in its path.

4. In this fourth stage of the fire intense heat is developed with temperatures soaring up to 1,700 degrees Fahrenheit. Materials that are combustible explode, which helps to spread the fire. Unless the fire can be extinguished here, major losses will occur within minutes.

On the bright side of the picture, man has developed some defenses against fire that are sophisticated and formidable. First of all, it is obvious that the best time to act on a fire is while it is in the incipient stage. Detection at this early stage should result in relatively easy extinguishing and minor damage.

Ionization Smoke-Detectors ───────────────────────────

The ionization smoke-detector is a popular early-warning device and enjoys the reputation of being the fastest known way of detecting fire in the incipient stage. This detector reacts to smoke and certain invisible particles of combustion. When sufficient particles are present an alarm in the detector is activated. (Figure 36.) The Fenwal Model CPD-1212 shown in the photograph is a dual-chamber ionization smoke-detector designed to sense both visible and invisible products of combustion (smoke and toxic gases). Solid-state, low-voltage circuitry with self-contained alarm and supervisory relays provide compatibility with most alarm system controls and accessories. The detector's sensitivity levels can be tested with a voltmeter.

The unit's operating conditions are indicated at the detector by an LED. Normal operation is indicated by a stable flash at approximately one flash per second. A loss of flash rate indicates a lessening of power or an open circuit; a constant light indicates the detector is in an alarm condition.

The detector measures 3¾ inches (9.54 cm) in height and 6¾ inches (16.8 cm) in width. The manufacturer warns that this detector should not be installed near areas with excessive exhaust fumes, kitchen areas, fireplaces, furnace rooms, or within 3 feet (.91 m) of air-supply ducts or air diffusers.

Figure 36. An ionization smoke-detector, such as the Fenwal Model CPD-1212, is the fastest known detector of fire in the incipient stage. Photograph courtesy of Fenwal, Inc.

Sprinkler Systems

The water sprinkler is a time-tested and valuable fire-fighting system. When the temperature in an area rises to a preset level, it automatically sprinkles water in that area. Water sprinklers, however, do not necessarily react before a substantial fire has developed. By that time, smoke and toxic gases may have killed people and damaged art works.

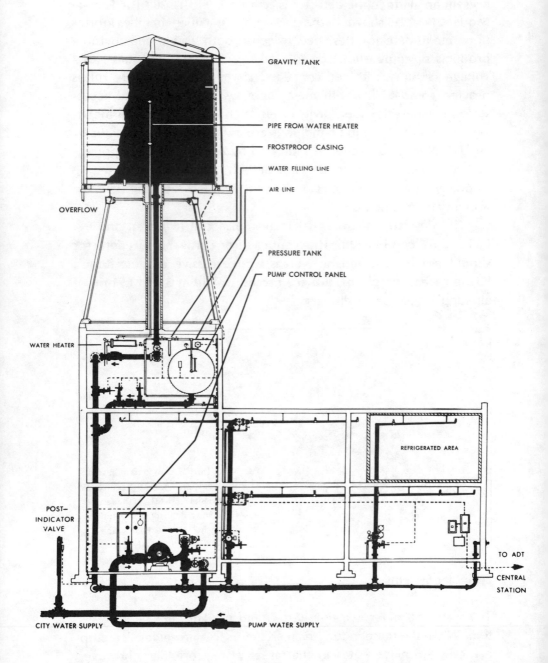

GRAVITY TANK

PIPE FROM WATER HEATER

FROSTPROOF CASING

WATER FILLING LINE

AIR LINE

OVERFLOW

PRESSURE TANK

PUMP CONTROL PANEL

WATER HEATER

REFRIGERATED AREA

POST-
INDICATOR
VALVE

TO ADT

CENTRAL
STATION

CITY WATER SUPPLY

PUMP WATER SUPPLY

Figure 37. When the temperature in a given area rises to a predetermined level, the sprinkler system is set off. Illustration courtesy of ADT.

Of course, sprinklers can mean other problems for the gallery or museum; namely, water damage to art. One method some museums have of solving this problem is to use the "dry"-type water sprinkler, which is designed to sprinkle water only at the location of the actual fire. This device is normally set to respond at 165 degrees Fahrenheit. Again, however, we are faced with the fact that by the time the heat has reached 165 degrees at the sprinkler heads, which are located in the ceiling, a very robust fire may have developed below. (Figure 37.) Supervisory devices are installed at all points of the sprinkler system that control the supply or distribution of water. These devices actuate transmitters which send a signal to a central station or to an in-plant protection headquarters. Circuits within the protected property and to the central station are under constant electrical supervision. Upon receiving a supervisory or trouble signal, central station personnel initiate the appropriate corrective action.

Abnormal conditions that would impair the effectiveness of a sprinkler system cause warning signals to be transmitted automatically. Furthermore, each device is protected against tampering and will initiate a signal whenever the cover of the housing is removed. The system instantly detects and reports the closing of a valve and maintains a constant check until it is reopened. It also automatically checks water levels and temperatures in gravity and pressure tanks and gives warning when either is low. It detects and reports dangerously high or low air pressure in pressure tanks and dry-pipe systems; also it detects and reports any critical variation below normal steam pressure for engine-driven fire pumps and any failure of electric power for fire pumps.

Other Fire Detectors

Additional types of fire fighters are listed below:

1. Flame detectors, which may be infrared or ultraviolet types, are capable of pinpointing just where the flame is located. These detectors are especially useful in storage areas where volatile materials are being used or stored.

2. Smoke detectors or photoelectric detectors discover a fire when it is in the stage where smoke is evident.

3. The line-type detector involves two twisted, stretched wires that are separated by low-melting-point insulation. When the tem-

perature reaches a predetermined level, the insulation melts, causing the wires to meet and trigger an alarm signal.

4. The rate-compensation detector is a combined rate-and-fixed-temperature device. The rate aspect of this detector is brought about by balancing the high heat expansion of the exterior covering against the inner, heat-shielded, low-expansion rods. When a fire develops it causes the exterior covering to heat up more rapidly than the hidden inner rods, closing an electrical contact. Then, when surrounding air attains a fixed, predetermined temperature, the exterior of the detector and the inner rods expand, the contacts close, and an alarm signal is triggered.

Hand-Held Extinguishers

Hand-held extinguishers containing carbon dioxide, Halon 1301 (an expensive liquified gas with an impressive safety-performance record), high-expansion foam, or water, are some of the available weapons for on-the-spot action in putting out fires. However, the museum personnel assigned to fire-fighting duties must be taught which type of extinguisher should be used to fight the various types of fire. The Underwriters' Laboratories states there are four kinds of fires, those that involve:

1. combustibles, which includes wood, cloth, and paper products;
2. gasoline, oil, grease, and other flammable chemicals;
3. electrical wiring;
4. combustible metals.

The museum fire-fighter should know that although water might be used to put out a paper fire, it could also electrocute the fire-fighter if used to fight an electrical fire; and, water used to put out a fire containing grease might cause an explosion.

Fire extinguishers are manufactured in different sizes. The sizes are indicated by number; the number 10 size being the largest and the number 2 size, the smallest. Fire extinguishers have to be serviced about twice a year or they may lose their effectiveness. Follow the manufacturer's maintenance instructions, which appear on the extinguisher.

Many museums have determined that a dual system is better suited for their fire-fighting purposes. They may use an early-warning smoke detector, to which the museum personnel respond with hand extinguishers. Should this course of action fail to put out the fire, then heat detectors activate automatic fire extinguishers and the fire department is alerted.

Every fire should be immediately reported to the fire department. It is very distressing to read about unsuccessful attempts to put out a fire by nonprofessionals. Certainly, attempts should be made to extinguish the fire by museum or gallery personnel, but not before the time has been taken to alert the fire department. A single example will graphically illustrate the need to notify the fire department immediately after a fire is detected. In July, 1978 a fire was touched off accidentally by a workman using an acetylene torch during restoration of New York City's historic St. Marks-in-the-Bowery Episcopal Church. The fire sent the roof crashing to the floor and shattered nine of the twenty-three stained glass windows in the 179-year-old church. A fire official attributed the extensive damage to the church to a ten-minute delay in turning on the fire alarm.

The following facts should be considered when developing a fire-fighting system:

1. Each fire-fighting system should be especially planned to meet the needs of a particular museum or gallery.

2. An expert in this specialized field should be enlisted to help design the system.

3. A training program for museum personnel should be organized to assure that they are prepared to respond effectively once a fire is detected. The local fire department should be able to assist in the training program and fire drills should be a part of this program. Frequent inspection of the fire-fighting equipment is critical to ensure that it is operational at all times and all equipment used should meet the basic standards of the National Fire Protection Association and the Underwriters' Laboratories. Some large museums, such as the Metropolitan Museum of Art in New York City, have their own fire departments.

5.
Security Against Vandalism

Vandalism is a disease felt by everybody in the international community. It is not predictable; even our cemeteries are not immune. Vandalism in museums and galleries usually occurs during business hours and is virtually not preventable.

Several such incidents come quickly to mind. One of these is the vandalization of Michelangelo's masterpiece *La Pieta*. This occurred when a man armed with a hammer suddenly struck out at the statue in Rome's glorious St. Peter's Cathedral. Over many months of arduous work, skilled craftsmen have done a remarkable job in restoring this famous sculpture. Then, too, the man who approached Picasso's *Guernica* in New York's Museum of Modern Art and sprayed red paint on the painting's surface was only temporarily successful. Happily, the Picasso canvas bore an excellent coat of varnish and immediate treatment by trained personnel saved the painting.

Clearly, as the following example indicates, the museum must have a plan devised to cope with the vandal's destructive inclinations. Failure to have such a program could bring disastrous results: Years ago, a crazed person threw fluid at a Sir Peter Paul Rubens painting that was displayed in a German museum. In the ensuing confusion the canvas was ignored for many hours. When the fluid was finally tested, it was found to be a paint remover whose chemical activity continues for many hours after application. The Rubens painting thus suffered deep, penetrating damage. The sad fact is that immediate action to identify and remove the fluid would have resulted in only minimal damage to the canvas.

In October, 1977 a man used a syringe to spray sulfuric acid on four paintings, one of which was Rembrandt's *Jacob's Blessing*, which were all on exhibit in the Wilhelmstoehe Palace Museum in Kassel, West Germany. There was much concern that the sprayed paintings had suffered irreparable damage. However, on January 19, 1978 a New Jersey newspaper, *The Record*, printed a joyful Associated Press release, which stated that the paintings were being restored in Düsseldorf and Munich, West Germany. "Chances for optimal restoration are very good," said Hubertus Falker von Sonnenburg, head of Munich's Doerner Institute.

The cases of vandalism go on. At the National Gallery in London, England a vandal slashed a Nicolas Poussin seventeenth-century painting entitled *Adoration of the Golden Calf,* leaving a gaping 3-foot hole in the canvas. In the April 4, 1978 issue the *New York Times* noted that "museum officials said they were confident the work could be restored. Its value is estimated at $925,000." In this instance a security guard apprehended the vandal.

On April 5, 1978 at the Municipal Museum in Amsterdam, Holland a vandal used a knife to slash Vincent Van Gogh's *La Berceuse.* Although the man was apprehended by guards, the *New York Daily News* reported the next day that the damage was very great and that it would take many months to restore the painting. The painting's value was estimated at 425 thousand dollars.

And lastly, on April 25, 1978 Amsterdam was the scene of another act of vandalism against a Van Gogh painting called *Self Portrait in Gray Hat.* According to the *New York Times'* April 26, 1978 edition, "A Dutch artist recently discharged from a mental hospital pulled out a knife today and slashed a Van Gogh self-portrait from corner to corner in an Amsterdam Museum, officials said." The estimated value of the painting was $1.5 million.

The cases cited here are not meant to shock or sadden, but rather to point out the severity of the problem.

Some museums respond to these acts of vandalism by placing more and more of their especially valuable art works under glass or Plexiglas. Some art observers believe that in the next decade or two going to a museum will be similar to visiting an aquarium—everything will be behind glass.

Security experts are aware of the great variety of electronic devices available to the museum to protect its treasures against theft, but those devices may not be the answer against the swift and destructive action of the vandal. The interval between the time the security device indicates an object has been removed or disturbed and the time it takes to send personnel from a central station on or off the premises to check out an intrusion may be too great to effect an apprehension or to stop the vandal's destruction.

The most efficient weapon against the vandal is the museum guard. The guard, hopefully, will witness the vandal's action. If the guard's attention is diverted, he should, at least have the advantage of an alarm system to assist him. Preferably, the device should issue an audible alarm, allowing the guard to pinpoint the area of intrusion, so that the response can be fast and decisive. There are such tools available and it is conceivable they can be used effectively by the guard in his efforts to combat the vandal.

The installation of step or pressure mats concealed beneath the carpeting is a relatively inexpensive, but effective, warning system. Installed in the area between the art object and the familiar cordon of velvet ropes, mats can trigger an alarm when stepped on, thus giving the guard a chance to reach the vandal before he strikes. In addition to sounding the alarm in the area of violation, the step mat can be installed so that the alarm is also received at the central monitoring point within the museum. This is solid backup coverage and is recommended.

To complement the concealed mat every museum should issue its guards two-way portable FM radios. The two-way portable FM radio permits instant communication with the security console or other guards, thus assuring the guard assistance in an emergency situation.

Once an act of vandalism has occurred, the local police should be advised immediately.

6.
Major Electronic
Security Systems

There are some incredibly complicated, yet fascinating, security systems being produced today. Some will protect the perimeter and interior of a home, gallery, or an entire museum whether occupied or not. Any violation of the system is reported electronically to a central station which records the incident and spews out information concerning remedial action to be taken. By the same token, the market is also being inundated with less expensive integrated security systems to handle the staggering increases in residential break-ins.

Let us turn now to have a look at some of these products.

The Central Station

The central alarm station can be used to monitor incoming signals from galleries and museums, as well as banks, jewelry stores, warehouses, and private homes.

The remote sensory devices trigger an alarm signal at the central station, and security supervisors take immediate action notifying local police or fire departments or dispatching alarm investigators to the emergency location. The incoming alarm signal indicating an emergency situation is flashed on a display screen and recorded by high-speed printer. At the same time, emergency information is retrieved from the computer's memory and similarly displayed, telling the security supervisor the location of the endangered premises, the appropriate emergency steps to be taken, and the telephone numbers of staff personnel, police, and fire departments to be called. (Figure 38.)

Figure 38. A fully automated, computerized control station has been developed by ADT. Photograph courtesy of ADT.

In the event that several alarms are received simultaneously, the computer will instantly put them in order of priority, and within seconds all will be displayed.

A Fully Automated Security and Building Management System

An example of a fully automated, on-site security and building-management system for a large building or multi-building complex is ADT's Centrascan 73 system. The system is based on a central-computer processing unit, receiving signals from remote sensory devices. It instantly handles information on a wide range of premises-protection and process-control situations. (Figure 39.) The nerve center of the system is its integrated command console, to which alarm signals are relayed from a variety of sensory and detection devices, and from which control signals may be sent automatically to remote actuators.

The computer is programmed according to the specific requirements of the building or group of buildings. The programming includes schedules of anticipated events, such as times when the doors are accessed and/or secured; electrical machinery start/stop commands in accordance with building occupancy patterns; equipment cycling for better use of energy; and preplanned, automatic responses to emergency situations. Also contained in the data base are action programs that are retrieved and displayed at the console in the event of an emergency. These programs provide building management or security personnel with complete sets of instructions for countering any number of problems. In case of a fire, for example, the system is designed to detect early stages of the blaze by means of electronic smoke detectors, which instantaneously react and trigger an alarm signal at the console. Here, the emergency is displayed on a lamp annunciator module which pinpoints its location. Simultaneously, to prevent or minimize losses the computer will initiate a series of automatic procedures. To discourage spread of smoke or sparks

Figure 39. ADT's Centrascan 73 is an example of a fully automated, on-site security and building-management system.

through building ducts, air handling equipment in the affected zones will be automatically shut down via a signal from the console. At the command console a CRT (cathode ray tube) will display all critical operating conditions, as well as a remedial action program, indicating in order of priority the steps to take in preventing or limiting losses. In the event of a fire, this computer-generated program will indicate fire department telephone numbers to contact, instructions for evacuation of the endangered area, lists of files and other records to be removed, and similar emergency information. The system may also be programmed for automatic release of magnetically actuated door latches, providing access for fire fighters.

As both emergency signals and routine signals are received at the console, they are recorded by a high-speed alphanumeric printer, along with the emergency action program as displayed on the CRT screen. The console operator's response to each instruction may also be recorded at the console, thus providing a permanent record of the incident. In handling routine signals, the system processes incoming access/secure information automatically on a management-by-exception basis. By taking over the processing and recording of routine signals, the system helps free security personnel to concentrate on nonroutine signals which indicate problems requiring immediate attention.

For fail-safe operation the system has the option of a redundant computer system with automatic switch-over in case of malfunction or failure of the primary unit. Additionally, the system is supported by a secondary power source, automatically actuated by the computer for continuing operation in the event of a power failure.

Site-engineered to the specific needs of a building or building complex, the system may be supplemented with CCTV surveillance monitors, and a videotape recorder at the command console. Similarly, the system's capabilities may be further expanded through the addition of paging and two-way-radio communications systems, as well as electronic card-access systems.

The system can also be set up so that the command console installed at the protected property is connected to the computer at a central alarm station, time-shared with other users. This arrangement provides high security and the advantages of flexible operation. Typically, this arrangement allows for on-premises operation of the system during selected time periods with off-premises monitoring at other times.

The Integrated Security System

The majority of burglaries today are committed by the impulsive intruder and not the highly sophisticated criminal, who plans every detail of his crime with great care and intelligence. The professional burglar is capable of defeating even the very complicated security-intrusion systems. In fact, his talents for bypassing electronic security systems seem to keep pace with the manufacturing of new systems. Although a great variety of highly sophisticated equipment has been developed, no system yet devised is guaranteed to be perfect; nor has a system been discovered which cannot be bypassed by a technically knowledgeable, professional criminal.

Nevertheless, it is the impulsive burglar who is responsible for most thefts. He is usually a young man, about eighteen years old. His planning, for the most part, is crude. He is interested in stealing property that can be quickly turned into cash by sale to a local "fence." The property he steals frequently includes cameras, cash, electric typewriters, guns, stereo and television sets, and, in most recent years, art objects. This type of crime is committed quickly, usually in less than ten minutes. In the United States a burglary occurs every twelve seconds. In fact, residential burglary is well up over fifty percent in the last five years—fifty-six percent of the burglaries taking place during the daytime hours.

The manufacturers of security products have attempted to counter this "quick crime technique" by producing devices that sound alarms inside and immediately outside the premises, hoping that the criminal will leave before completing the theft. It is also hoped that the alarm will attract a neighbor, passerby, or patrol car. This type of security device is often referred to as the "integrated security system." It breaks away from the more expensive systems which are linked to police or central stations. Most of the integrated systems are installed by simply plugging them into an outlet.

The Ultrason-X Burglar Alarm, manufactured by the Master Lock Company, is typical of the type of system that has been developed to combat the "quick crime technique" of the unsophisticated burglar. (Figure 40.) It is an ultrasonic device that is installed by merely plugging it into any 120-volt outlet. The system emits an ultrasonic field of about 30 feet (9 m). When the intruder enters the ultrasonic field, his presence causes an audible alarm to be sounded (and triggers lights, in some instances). Another important feature is the satellite.

Figure 40. The Ultrason-X Alarm has been developed to fight the unsophisticated burglar. The cube-shaped satellite is on the right. The system has been designed to attractively blend with home decor. Photograph courtesy of Master Lock Co.

The cube-shaped, hand-sized satellite can be easily carried to a neighbor's home if the owner is going out. There it can be plugged into an outlet. If an intrusion occurs in the owner's home, the alarm will sound in the owner's home and in the home where the satellite has been installed, as well. Not only will the burglar be shocked by the alarm blaring at him in the residence, but the neighbor will be able to notify the police. The satellite can also be used in a separate room of the home. The intruder will then actuate loud alarms in two rooms. Hopefully, the intruder will become sufficiently frightened and will leave the premises before completing the burglary; or, as they might say in England, "has it away on his toes."

The integrated security system described here is 10⅝ inches wide, 3½ inches high, and 6 inches deep (27 by 8.9 by 15.24 cm). It sells for $180. The satellites come in two models; the louder satellite is recommended and it's available for $43.

The Crime Fighter Alarm is another type of inexpensive device developed by Master Lock to scare off the unsophisticated burglar. (Figure 41.) The solid-state alarm warns of an intrusion with a loud, shrieking siren. The panic-button included with each system is always armed, around the clock. But, if an intruder enters while the burglar circuit is turned off, pressing the panic switch will still sound an instant alarm to alert neighbors and drive off the intruder. Once the siren is set off by an intruder, he can't silence it by simply closing the door or window or by cutting sensor wires. The homeowner must turn it off from a hidden control.

All parts of the system are prewired with connectors that simply plug together like the components of a stereo radio for fast, easy installation. The unit itself sells for about one hundred dollars. One 12-volt battery (not included) supplies all the power required.

A Residential Fire and Burglary System

For the homeowner who decides to invest in a complete burglary and fire security system the ADT System 7575 is typical. The system combines protection against intrusion with early-warning fire detection. It is installed to provide on-site warning signals or, if desired, may be connected to a central alarm station.

The central station service adds an extra dimension of security, providing for twenty-four-hour-a-day, off-premises monitoring while residents are at home or away. Fire- and intrusion-alarm signals triggered by the system are designed to alert central station personnel, who summon police or fire fighters.

The nerve center is a control panel which technicians install in a convenient, central location in the home; generally, a front hallway near the entrance. This control is secured by a lock, thereby allowing only the home's occupants or other authorized key holders to activate and deactivate the system. (Figure 42.) Also incorporated in this control panel are an emergency button for sounding a warning signal within the home or for sending a "silent alarm" to the central station; lamp displays, which tell when secured doors and windows are closed and protection is "on"; and a reset switch to reactivate fire alarm smoke-detectors, following a test or actual fire.

Connected to the control panel are a series of remote detection devices that are designed to react to emergencies as they occur. The number and variety of sensors included with the system should be determined by the size of the home and the desired degree of protection. Included are magnetic contact sets, pressure mats, ultrasonic units, and photoelectric sensors.

Smoke detectors are ceiling-mounted in strategic spots, including stairwell areas, kitchens, and other locations in the home where fire is apt to start or where smoke will be conveyed by normal household air movements. Sensing the very early beginnings of a home fire, which are generally accompanied by heavy concentrations of smoke, these units will sound a loud alarm at the control panel or at a remote outdoor speaker. A portable, wireless alarm device may be carried in pocket, purse, or on your belt and will send an alarm from any spot in the home or from nearby areas, such as a garage or driveway.

Where added in-home alarm signalling is desired, a weatherproof outdoor loudspeaker provides for a loud signal to alert residents or neighbors to fire or intrusion attempts. If desired, a bedroom emergency-button unit, containing an alarm-sounding device, may be added to the system to allow a resident to signal for assistance in the event of intrusion, a medical emergency, or other problem.

Figure 42. A residential fire and burglary security system control panel. Photograph courtesy of ADT.

7.
The Reality of Art Thefts

The security systems described in this book are impressively sophisticated, reflecting tremendous technological advances in the field of security. The cold, hard facts are these, however: statistically, a certain number of art thefts and acts of destruction will occur each year, regardless of the security systems used. That leaves the art collector or institution with the problems of how to deal with these unfortunate acts once they've occurred.

Insurance

The most obvious step, of course, is to insure the art objects against theft, vandalism, and damage. The problem here is that the number of art thefts, which continues to increase each year, has pushed the cost of insurance to new heights. In discussing business conditions with art gallery owners over the past ten years, the high cost of insurance has always been a disheartening topic. Some galleries said the costs have become so prohibitive that they are considering doing without insurance. Most galleries lease their places of business, and the combined overhead of rent, utilities, salaries, and insurance make it difficult to maintain a profitable enterprise.

In addition to the high cost, many conscientious people employed in the fine-arts insurance business readily admit that there are loopholes that need closing up within the insurance industry. For example, the author is familiar with a case whereby an insurance agent wrote up a policy amounting to approximately one-quarter million dollars for a small art gallery. The agent did not obtain a detailed inventory of the art objects he had insured and he did not request photographs of any of the objects. A theft was reported and the gallery owners claimed all the art had been stolen. The owners apparently could not produce any photographs, bills of sale, or even adequate descriptions of the missing objects. Furthermore, they claimed to have never prepared a catalogue of these gallery art objects. Thus, the insurance company and the investigative agencies were left with only the barest of details about the property they were attempting to recover, and the insurance company was confronted with the distinct possibility of having to pay a claim amounting to approximately 250 thousand dollars.

Did the insurance agent who wrote the expensive policy do so for monetary gain alone? Shouldn't the insurance companies, as an industry, have certain standards that would prevent a situation like the one described here? The author believes that were such standards to be set the potential savings would more than compensate for the additional administrative costs of implementing such a system. These standards should include instructions that insurance agents obtain complete inventories and photographs of the property being insured.

Conversations with officials of several insurance companies specializing in fine arts reveal that they reserve the right to refuse to insure a gallery, museum, or collector if the security is not adequate. They agreed that while it is true that insurance rates have risen because of the high incidence of art thefts in the past, the rising value of art has also played a very significant role in the increased costs.

For one reason or another, museums have been faced with tremendous problems concerning their insurance rates. In fact, the cost of insuring travelling art exhibitions, particularly those that travel internationally, has risen to such heights that some museums have actually stopped participating in this important area.

There is a brighter side to this picture, however. The United States Government now indemnifies travelling art exhibits under the Arts and Artifacts Indemnity Act. This act was passed into law on December 20, 1975, as Public Law 94-158, 94th Congress, S. 1800. Briefly, the act states that the federal government will indemnify works of art involved in travelling exchange exhibitions against loss or damage. Applications are made to, and must be approved by, the Department of State. The agency charged with the administration of this act is the Federal Council on the Arts and Humanities.

In a report to Congress on January 5, 1978, Joseph D. Duffey, Chairman of the Federal Council on the Arts and Humanities, said that:

> In fiscal year 1977 the Federal Council approved 17 applications for indemnities and one application to amend an Indemnity Certificate. Approved indemnities totalled $131,626,121 for 3,906 objects included in 17 different exhibitions. Based on the figures from indemnitees, it is estimated that the amount of premiums they would have paid to insure these exhibitions commercially is $1,516,525. . . .
>
> No claims were received by the Federal Council from any of its indemnitees. The planning, handling and security of indemnified objects provided by the hundreds of foreign lenders and museum curators in this country, as well as packing and shipping agents was extraordinary.

There appears to be little that the consumer can do in general about the high cost of insuring art, except to pay the premiums. There is no indication that insurance prices are going to decrease in the foreseeable future. However, all is not lost! There are some areas where money may be saved without decreasing coverage. For one thing, on every piece of commercial property in the United States, which includes galleries and museums, there is an established fire insurance rate. And, since the fire insurance rate is the single most important factor in determining the amount of the overall insurance premium, it might be beneficial for museum and gallery administrators to frequently review this aspect of their insurance. Insist that the insurance underwriter or broker inspect the premises periodically. It is possible he could make some money-saving suggestions, such as that of adding fire extinguishers in strategic areas or installing extra smoke detectors. And, if the museum has added a complete building security system, including fire-fighting equipment, it is clear that some beneficial adjustments to policy holder's premiums are indicated. It is also clear that frequent liaison with the insurance man, keeping him informed of any changes in the operation of the museum, should become standard operating procedure for museum administrators.

Once a work of art has been stolen, does that mean that it is lost forever? Not necessarily, is the answer.

The following comments concerning the recovery of stolen art are based upon personal experience:

1. The recovery rate for well-known works is far greater than for lesser-known works.

2. Some art is recovered a few days after the theft.

3. Some works are missing for many years as in the case of the El Greco modello, *The Immaculate Conception*, which was stolen from a villa outside of Madrid in 1936 and recovered in New York City in 1971.

4. Interestingly, some art is recovered before the owners are aware that a theft has occurred.

5. According to the French National Police and experienced investigators in the United States, generally, stolen art is recovered within five years after the theft, if it is to be recovered at all.

Over the years, the author has frequently been asked, "Does the FBI have jurisdiction in art cases?" or, put more bluntly, "What's the FBI doing investigating art thefts?" The answer is that, according to federal law, the FBI is authorized to conduct such investigations and does have jurisdiction in certain cases. Generally, the FBI has primary jurisdiction in theft cases where the property is valued at five thousand dollars or more.

In practice, there are four federal laws under which art thefts and art fraud cases are investigated by the FBI. They are Sections 2314, 2315, 1343, and 659 of Title 18, United States Code. The pertinent parts of these laws are set forth below:

Section 2314—Transportation of stolen goods, securities, moneys, fraudulent state tax stamps, or articles used in counterfeiting:

Whoever transports in interstate or foreign commerce any goods, wares, merchandise (art, for example), securities or money, of the value of $5,000 or more, knowing the same to have been stolen, converted or taken by fraud; or

Whoever, having devised or intending to devise any scheme or artifice to defraud, or for obtaining money or property by means of false or fraudulent pretenses, representations, or promises, transports or causes to be transported, or induces any person to travel in, or to be transported in interstate commerce in the execution or concealment of a scheme or artifice to defraud that person of money or property having a value of $5,000 . . . shall be fined not more than $10,000 or imprisoned not more than ten years or both.

Section 2315—Sale or receipt of stolen goods, securities, moneys, or fraudulent state tax stamps:

Whoever receives, conceals, stores, barters, sells, or disposes of any goods, wares, or merchandise, securities, or money of the value of $5,000 or more, or pledges or accepts as security for a loan any goods, wares or merchandise, or securities, of the value of $500 or more, moving as, or which are a part of, or which constitute interstate or foreign commerce, knowing the same to have been stolen, unlawfully converted or taken . . . shall be fined not more than $10,000 or imprisoned not more than ten years, or both.

Sections 2314 and 2315 are commonly referred to by the FBI as Interstate Transportation of Stolen Property or ITSP violations cases. These are the two federal laws under which the majority of art theft and art fraud cases are investigated by the FBI.

Section 659—Theft from interstate shipment—is similar in structure to Sections 2314 and 2315 in that it pertains to interstate or foreign commerce of stolen property. The major difference, though, is that this law concentrates on the theft of property while it is being transported in interstate or foreign commerce by a common carrier (such as a truck). Another significant difference between Sections 2314, 2315, and 659 is value. You will recall that value in Sections 2314 and 2315 is five thousand dollars or more; under Section 659 the necessary value is one hundred dollars or more.

Section 659 is additionally broken down into two main sections—theft and possession. Under the possession section, guilty knowledge must be established before prosecution. However, guilty knowledge can be implied if the theft occurred shortly before the arrest. In practice, the period of time passing between the theft and the arrest should probably be seventy-two hours or less. Any time more than that and the theft becomes difficult to prosecute; possession cases are becoming increasingly more difficult to prosecute.

An interesting phase of this law is the sentence, which is the same for theft or possession, namely, five thousand dollars fine and/or ten years imprisonment. However, under the possession section, if the property is not valued at over one hundred dollars, the maximum penalty is one thousand dollars fine and/or one year in prison.

Section 1343, Title 18 (USC)—Fraud by wire, radio or television—is often used by the FBI to investigate art fraud cases. This law states that:

> It is unlawful to devise any scheme or artifice to defraud or for obtaining money or property by means of false or fraudulent pretenses, representations or promises, transmit or cause to be transmitted by means of wire, radio or television, in interstate or foreign commerce, any writing, signs, signals, pictures or sounds for the purpose of executing such scheme or artifice shall be fined not more than $1,000 or imprisoned not more than 5 years.

The International Guide to Missing Treasures

Regardless of who is investigating the crime, the recovery of stolen art has been further complicated by the fact that there is no central filing system in the United States for these thefts. While serving as a special agent of the Federal Bureau of Investigation, the author made several official suggestions to the National Crime Information Center (NCIC) to include stolen works of art in its program. The requests were all denied.

The NCIC is an FBI-managed, vast computer center in Washington, D.C. It is a nationwide network that receives information by teletype from the police agencies of the United States concerning wanted individuals and stolen property, such as guns, automobiles, cameras, securities—almost any property, but not art. Law enforcement authorities in England and France have computerized their art thefts for some years now and have been encouraged by the results. While aware of the need, the NCIC has not found a working solution for entering this complex category of stolen property into its system, but does have the problem under consideration. It is believed that in time the NCIC will be able to expand its facilities to include art thefts.

Meanwhile, the lack of a central reporting-service for stolen art remains the great inhibitor to the art-theft investigator; and, because there has not been such a service for the institution or private collector to consult, they may be unknowingly participating in the purchase or sale of stolen art objects. This problem has been challenged by the recent introduction of a publication and service called, "The International Guide to Missing Treasures," (IGMT) 219 East 69th Street, New York, New York 10021. Two New York City art dealers, Lynn Epsteen and Ronald Feldman, along with the author, have just begun publication of the IGMT, which will report the world's missing art. The list will include paintings, drawings, sculpture, prints, ethnological art, antiquities, antiques, rare coins and books, tapestries, and manuscripts.

In addition to cataloging and publishing information concerning missing art works, the "Guide" offers a service to its subscribers. In the event of a reported loss, a "News Bulletin" will be dispatched to the international art community, police agencies, and subscribers concerning the missing work. The IGMT will publish only those art works that have been reported missing to the police.

The IGMT may prove its usefulness to the law in more subtle ways than merely as a central index for stolen art. The recorded art theft in the IGMT may ultimately stand as evidence in establishing ownership of an art work.

The July 16, 1978 edition of the *New York Times* in a story titled "Georgia O'Keeffe Loses Stolen-Paintings Lawsuit," reported that:

> In a case with potentially wide ramifications in the art
> world, Georgia O'Keeffe, the painter, lost her court battle
> to regain possession of three small paintings of hers that
> were stolen 32 years ago.
>
> Judge Hervey Moore of Mercer County Court in Trenton
> (New Jersey) said that O'Keeffe "slept on her rights for 30
> years and failed to take action that may have been
> productive."

The O'Keeffe case has wide ramifications, as it poses critical legal questions. Can one steal a painting, hide it for twenty years, and then claim it legally? Would the O'Keeffe decision have been made in her favor if a publication like the IGMT had been available and used by O'Keeffe to enter a description of her stolen paintings thirty-two years ago? Would this action, along with reporting the theft to a law enforcement agency, provide the necessary "productive action" the judge mentioned and thus help to establish ownership of a work of art?

8.
A Guide to
Decreasing Art Thefts

While there are no sure-fire solutions to the problems created by art thefts, art collectors may well find the suggestions that follow worthy of consideration.

Suggestions for the Private Collector _____

1. Deal only with reputable people.
2. Avoid "bargains." They may prove to be expensive fakes or stolen works.
3. If you are inexperienced, contact your local museum, art association, or chamber of commerce for information regarding reliable dealers.
4. If you have questions about the authenticity of an art work, contact your nearest museum for advice. The Art Dealers Association of America, Inc., 575 Madison Avenue, New York, New York, and the International Foundation for Art Research, Inc., 24 East 81st Street, New York, New York 10028, are widely known for their efforts in protecting the consumer from purchasing fraudulent works of art.
5. Photograph your collection and prepare a detailed inventory. Leave copies of the photographs and inventory with your attorney or in a safe-deposit box. One New York City collector reported a million-dollar art theft, and, to make things worse, the thieves also stole the collector's detailed inventory of his collection.
6. Be sure your insurance coverage grows with your collection. Consult your insurance agent as you make additions to your collection. Remind him that your collection probably is increasing in value each year.
7. If you have a message-answering device to take calls, do not

leave detailed information about your itinerary. Be vague. Use such phrases as "I will return soon," as opposed to "I will be away for the entire day, but will return home tomorrow morning at 11:00 A.M."

8. Maintain frequent contact with the firm that has installed your security system. Have your system checked frequently to determine if you are getting maximum coverage for your money; and, oh yes, do not forget to turn it on!

If you do not have a security system in your residence, consider shopping carefully for one now and have it installed as soon as possible. Time is not on your side! There is a security system available for every budget. If you have any questions as to what system is adequate for you, contact a security consultant.

9. If you plan to be away, employ a trusted neighbor or relative to keep an eye on your residence. Before leaving, stop deliveries of milk, newspapers, and mail. Be certain to leave your home adequately illuminated while you are away; use automatic timers to turn your lights on and off. Some automatic timers have the capability of turning your lights on or off at varied times. You may use the automatic timers in the same manner with your radios or television sets. Notify your local police department about your departure and return. If you plan to be away for an extended period of time, consider storing your collection in a bonded warehouse.

10. Think about the security of your valuables. Would you leave fifty thousand dollars in cash unguarded in your home? Obviously, the answer is no. Then why would you not take similar precautions to protect your fifty thousand dollars worth of art?

Suggestions for the Gallery, Museum, or Library

Many of the suggestions made to the collector also apply to the gallery, museum, and library. Additional suggestions follow:

1. Make sure that your employees do not permit visitors to wander around without being observed constantly. Visitors should be asked to leave their umbrellas, packages, or valises with the receptionist or in a supervised coat room.

2. Do not leave valuable property of visitors unguarded. A New York City gallery recently had two valuable fur coats stolen from its coat room. A common ploy of the thief is to distract your attention while a companion commits the theft.

3. Do not leave valuable small works of art near exit doors.

4. Properly secure valuable small paintings or sculptures that are being exhibited. Many galleries and museums display their small valuable works in locked glass or clear plastic cases.

5. Consider keeping the front door locked during business hours and admitting only those persons you believe to be reliable. This is a common practice among New York City galleries. Some galleries take this one step further. While the visitor is standing at the door waiting to be admitted, the gallery employee looks at the visitor and if he is recognized or if he appears to be reliable, pushes a button, which then electrically releases the door bolt and permits access. The reader may find these security measures repugnant and excessive and certainly not an ordinary way to welcome visitors to a business establishment. Call it a sign of the times, if you will, but the system does afford a degree of security and is especially reassuring to the lone person who we often find running an art gallery.

6. Maintain a thorough and accurate inventory of all museum art work, particularly pieces in stock.

The vulnerability of small paintings cannot be overlooked. During a visit to London in 1977, the author observed one art dealer who protected a row of his valuable small paintings in an unusual, but effective manner. He linked them together with a brass chain and locks.

According to Donald Langton, a retired New Scotland Yard art investigator, a large number of small paintings were stolen off the walls of London's museums and galleries, including the Queen's Galleries in Buckingham Palace and Hampton Court, which are open to the public. The thefts of the paintings, some of which included works by Picasso, Lautrec, Modigliani, Saeftleven, and Renoir usually occurred during lunchtime when staffs were depleted. An inquiry into the nature of these thefts determined that none of the premises involved had made provisions to secure the paintings to the wall; nearly all of the stolen paintings had been hung in those parts of the galleries which were poorly illuminated and out of view of the staff. A subsequent campaign advising galleries and museums to secure their paintings to the walls and to avoid placing the paintings in dark corners has greatly reduced this type of theft.

Museum and gallery administrators should consider another important step and that is the making of certain changes in their shipping practices. Unknowingly, they may be making their property too tempting for the criminal. Two particular cases come to mind where museums suffered major thefts while paintings they had shipped disappeared at John F. Kennedy Airport in New York. When recovered in New York by the FBI, an examination of the shipping crates made it apparent why the thieves thought the articles inside the crates might be worth stealing. On the upper lefthand corner of the crate were the museum's full name and address. Also stencilled in large block letters were such eye-catching statements as VALU-ABLE—OIL PAINTINGS—FRAGILE—DON'T DROP. Surely, museums and galleries can achieve shipment of their objects with less flair and more discretion. Why invite a thief to act?

The Importance of Protecting Art Inventories _____

As far as inventories are concerned, the author feels that too little has been done to protect the great and tremendously valuable collections of our institutions. A dramatic case comes to mind.

In 1977 the Detroit Institute of Arts was staggered by the theft of over four hundred thousand dollars worth of art objects from its inventory. A handyman, who had worked for the museum for fourteen years, was arrested and charged with receiving and concealing the stolen museum property. It was suspected that the art objects had been removed from the museum's reserve inventory over a period of many years.

Usually, in a case like this, the theft is not discovered until a reserve item is requested; and, since museums often do not do complete inventories for years, it is possible for a theft to go unnoticed for an extensive period of time. In a large institution it is not unusual for an inventory to take six months to complete, with perhaps twenty people involved in the work on a full-time schedule. It is apparent that museums simply do not believe they can afford to release the necessary number of employees to conduct more frequent inventories; nor do they feel they can afford to hire outside personnel to perform this vital task.

Surely, museums must come up with a workable idea concerning the protection of their inventories. One museum administrator had a unique approach to this problem. He felt it might become necessary to ask federal authorities to consider storing museum inventories in a central repository (sort of a Fort Knox of art). The inconvenience of such a system makes it impractical, though it is an interesting idea. The industry itself, possibly through a museum association, should organize a committee to study this problem and make appropriate recommendations. The United States Government may prove to be receptive to lending a powerful hand, as it did with the passage of the Arts and Artifacts Indemnity Act.

The Detroit inventory theft case highlighted still another problem facing the American public today and that is the controversy raging about seemingly light sentences for serious crimes. This controversy perpetuates itself when we read newspaper articles such as the one about the Detroit inventory case appearing in the *New York Post* on July 6, 1977. The article, titled "425G Art Thefts Net $200 Fine," stated that "a Detroit Institute of Arts handyman who helped steal $425,000 in artwork—including pieces by Picasso and Rubens— was fined $200 yesterday and placed on two years' probation."

Special Suggestions for Libraries

Security problems are not restricted to the collector, gallery, or museum, however. Libraries and archives are facing similar problems with a rising incidence of theft. The thieves seem to concentrate on rare books and often cut or rip out valuable prints from books. They pilfer manuscripts, documents, letters, and envelopes; they are interested not only in letters signed by the famous, but also in envelopes bearing rare postmarks.

A recent theft of manuscripts comes to mind. In August of 1977 George Washington's Revolutionary War Headquarters at Newburgh, New York, reported a theft of documents that related to Washington's stay at his headquarters. Also stolen were papers concerning shippirating on the Hudson River during the American Revolution. Another example was the loss in 1977 of a very valuable stamp collection by a branch of the New York Public Library. In fact, the ALA (American Library Association) is very concerned about spiraling library thefts, and the author was privileged to speak on the problem at the ALA National Convention in Detroit in 1977.

The adequacy of the protection of any institution is usually governed by the resources of that institution. The following are techniques and suggestions, however, that may help tighten up library security and that do not necessarily involve a great deal of money:

1. Call slips should be used and filed in an efficient manner. They should be retained for a reasonable time for possible use as evidence.

2. Inventory of the library's most valuable objects on a very frequent basis is essential.

3. Staff members should be trained to be vigilant about their reference room supervision. The training program should include a plan of how to respond to a theft when it occurs. Instruction pertaining to the local theft laws should be part of the training program. The legal responsibilities of the staff member and the constitutional rights of the thief have to be clearly understood. If the staff has received proper training, it will feel more confident about its response when a theft occurs. (Some communities are using their shoplifting laws in connection with prosecution of library thieves.)

4. The feasibility of instituting admission by photo-identification card only should be considered.

5. All rare documents and books should be marked with an indelible marker. This is a very positive technique in helping to stop thefts. It may also stand as good proof of ownership. The author is well aware of the fact that these marking procedures are not universally accepted, as they may disfigure or alter the document's appearance to some degree, but current theft statistics dictate the utilization of this procedure.

6. A policy decision should be made as to what personal possessions the patron should be allowed to bring into the reading room.

7. Library rules should be posted in a clear manner so that the patron can follow the rules intelligently.

8. If the library can afford it, it should retain a security consultant. A list of consultants may be obtained from the Society of American Archivists Archival Security Program, Box 8198, University of Illinois, Chicago Circle, Chicago, Illinois 60680.

9. Local police authorities should be consulted about the security problems.

10. If the library inventory includes valuable paintings, sculpture, or other works of art, it should be made certain that these objects are afforded adequate security.

9.
What to Do if You Discover an Art Theft

The shock felt by a person when he first discovers a theft is numbing. A feeling of hopelessness follows, but there are certain steps that should be taken immediately following the discovery—steps that ultimately may lead to the recovery of the missing treasures.

1. Report the theft to the local police at once.

2. Do not disturb the scene of the crime. Try to keep it as it was found until the police arrive.

3. Consider publicizing the theft in the local news media.

4. Report the theft to the local office of the FBI and, even though they might not have jurisdiction in the case, ask them to record and index the details of the theft. Somebody, at some point, may ask them about such a theft and they may be able to help recover the property.

5. Immediately telephone all the people you know who are familiar with the missing treasures or who are knowledgeable in that particular field of art. This technique is used frequently in Europe and has been found to be effective during the first forty-eight hours following a theft, the span of time during which a thief often will try to sell his stolen wares.

6. Notify your insurance company and insist that photographs and a description of the missing property be forwarded to pertinent dealers, museums, and auction houses.

7. Consider sending photographs and descriptions of stolen works to the following organizations, who have experienced personnel working in the art theft recovery field:

Interpol, c/o U.S. Department of Justice, Washington, D.C. 20530, telephone (202) 739-2867

FBI Headquarters, Interstate Transportation of Stolen Property Desk, J. Edgar Hoover Building, Washington, D.C. 20535, telephone (202) 324-3000

FBI, Supervisor, Art Squad, 201 E. 69th St., New York, N.Y. 10021, telephone (212) 535-7700

New York City Police Department, Commanding Officer, Property Recovery Squad, 1 Police Plaza, New York, N.Y. 10038, telephone (212) 374-3823

Art Dealers Association of America, Inc., 575 Madison Ave., New York, N.Y. 10022, telephone (212) 644-7150.

8. By all means, please do not forget to send photographs and descriptions of your stolen property to the publication and service, "The International Guide to Missing Treasures," c/o the author, Donald L. Mason, at 219 E. 69th St., New York, N.Y. 10021, telephone (212) 753-2408.

Security Equipment Manufacturers

Ademco
165 Eileen Way
Syosset, N.Y. 11791

Advanced Devices Laboratory, Inc.
520 S. Rock Blvd.
Reno, Nev. 89502

Advanced Signaling Company, Inc.
P.O. Box 5841
Arlington, Tex. 76011

Alarm Products International, Inc.
24-02 40th Ave.
Long Island City, N.Y. 11101

American District Telegraph (ADT)
#1 World Trade Center, Suite 9200
New York, N.Y. 10048

Aritech Corp.
25 Newbury St.
Framingham, Mass. 02134

Audio Sentry Corp.
31807 Utica Rd.
Fraser, Mich. 48026

B-Safe Systems, Inc.
P.O. Box 28301
Atlanta, Ga. 30328

C. E. M. Security Products
916 W. Maude Ave.
Sunnyvale, Calif. 94086

Colorado Electro Optics, Inc.
1840 Commerce St.
Boulder, Colo. 80301

Conrac Corp.
Mill Rock Rd.
Old Saybrook, Conn. 06475

Contronic Controls Ltd.
7611 Bath Rd.
Mississauga, Ont. L4T 3TI, Canada

Defensive Security Corp.
158 Eileen Way
Syosset, N.Y. 11791

Detection Systems, Inc.
400 Mason Rd.
Fairport, N.Y. 14450

Detector Industries (Div. Binswanger Mirror)
P.O. Box 17127
Memphis, Tenn. 38117

Fenwald, Inc.
400 Main St.
Ashland, Mass. 01721

Fire Burglary Instruments, Inc.
999 A Stewart Ave.
Garden City, N.Y. 11530

Fire Control Instruments, Inc.
149 California St.
Newton, Mass. 02185

GTE Sylvania Security Systems
P.O. Box 188
Mountain View, Calif. 94042

Honeywell, Inc.
Honeywell Plaza
Minneapolis, Minn. 55408

Interstate Engineering (Div. A_T_O)
522 E. Vermont Ave.
Anaheim, Calif. 92805

Master Lock Co.
2600 N. 32nd St.
Milwaukee, Wis. 53210

Medeco
P.O. Box 1075
Salem, Va. 24153

Motorola Communications & Electronics, Inc.
1301 E. Algonquin Rd.
Schaumburg, Ill. 60196

Mountain West Alarm Supply Co.
P.O. Box 10780
Phoenix, Ariz. 85064

Poly-Scientific (Litton Systems, Inc.)
1213 N. Main St.
Blacksburg, Va. 24060

Power Sonic Corp.
P.O. Box 5242
Redwood City, Calif. 94063

RCA Electro Optics & Devices
Solid State Division
Lancaster, Pa. 17604

Raytek, Inc. (Div. Optical Coating Lab.)
325 E. Middlefield Rd.
Mountain View, Calif. 94043

Rockwell International
3370 Miraloma Ave.
Anaheim, Calif. 92803

Security World Publishing Co.
2639 S. La Cienega Blvd.
Los Angeles, Calif. 90034

Stellar Systems, Inc.
3020 Olcott St.
Santa Clara, Calif. 95051

Wells Fargo Alarm Services
1533 26th St.
Santa Monica, Calif. 90404

Western Alarm Supply Co.
1414 Blake St.
Denver, Colo. 80202

Index